"This series is a tremendous resource for t
understanding of how the gospel is wov(
pastors and scholars doing gospel business from an the ocaptor
logical feast preparing God's people to apply the entire Bible to all of life with heart and mind
wholly committed to Christ's priorities."

> **BRYAN CHAPELL,** President Emeritus, Covenant Theological Seminary; Senior Pastor,
> Grace Presbyterian Church, Peoria, Illinois

"Mark Twain may have smiled when he wrote to a friend, 'I didn't have time to write you a
short letter, so I wrote you a long letter.' But the truth of Twain's remark remains serious and
universal, because well-reasoned, compact writing requires extra time and extra hard work.
And this is what we have in the Crossway Bible study series *Knowing the Bible*. The skilled authors and notable editors provide the contours of each book of the Bible as well as the grand
theological themes that bind them together as one Book. Here, in a 12-week format, are care-
fully wrought studies that will ignite the mind and the heart."

> **R. KENT HUGHES,** Visiting Professor of Practical Theology, Westminster Theological
> Seminary

"*Knowing the Bible* brings together a gifted team of Bible teachers to produce a high-quality
series of study guides. The coordinated focus of these materials is unique: biblical content,
provocative questions, systematic theology, practical application, and the gospel story of God's
grace presented all the way through Scripture."

> **PHILIP G. RYKEN,** President, Wheaton College

"These *Knowing the Bible* volumes provide a significant and very welcome variation on the
general run of inductive Bible studies. This series provides substantial instruction, as well as
teaching through the very questions that are asked. *Knowing the Bible* then goes even further
by showing how any given text links with the gospel, the whole Bible, and the formation of
theology. I heartily endorse this orientation of individual books to the whole Bible and the
gospel, and I applaud the demonstration that sound theology was not something invented
later by Christians, but is right there in the pages of Scripture."

> **GRAEME L. GOLDSWORTHY,** former lecturer, Moore Theological College; author,
> *According to Plan*, *Gospel and Kingdom*, *The Gospel in Revelation*, and *Gospel and Wisdom*

"What a gift to earnest, Bible-loving, Bible-searching believers! The organization and structure
of the Bible study format presented through the *Knowing the Bible* series is so well conceived.
Students of the Word are led to understand the content of passages through perceptive, guided
questions, and they are given rich insights and application all along the way in the brief but
illuminating sections that conclude each study. What potential growth in depth and breadth
of understanding these studies offer! One can only pray that vast numbers of believers will
discover more of God and the beauty of his Word through these rich studies."

> **BRUCE A. WARE,** Professor of Christian Theology, The Southern Baptist Theological
> Seminary

KNOWING THE BIBLE

J. I. Packer, Theological Editor
Dane C. Ortlund, Series Editor
Lane T. Dennis, Executive Editor

•   •   •   •   •   •

Genesis	Psalms	Jonah, Micah, and Nahum	Ephesians
Exodus	Proverbs		Philippians
Leviticus	Ecclesiastes	Haggai, Zechariah, and Malachi	Colossians and Philemon
Numbers	Song of Solomon		
Deuteronomy	Isaiah	Matthew	1–2 Thessalonians
Joshua	Jeremiah	Mark	1–2 Timothy and Titus
Judges	Lamentations, Habakkuk, and Zephaniah	Luke	
Ruth and Esther		John	Hebrews
1–2 Samuel	Ezekiel	Acts	James
1–2 Kings	Daniel	Romans	1–2 Peter and Jude
1–2 Chronicles	Hosea	1 Corinthians	1–3 John
Ezra and Nehemiah	Joel, Amos, and Obadiah	2 Corinthians	Revelation
Job		Galatians	

•   •   •   •   •   •

J. I. PACKER was the former Board of Governors' Professor of Theology at Regent College (Vancouver, BC). Dr. Packer earned his DPhil at the University of Oxford. He is known and loved worldwide as the author of the best-selling book *Knowing God*, as well as many other titles on theology and the Christian life. He served as the General Editor of the ESV Bible and as the Theological Editor for the *ESV Study Bible*.

LANE T. DENNIS is CEO of Crossway, a not-for-profit publishing ministry. Dr. Dennis earned his PhD from Northwestern University. He is Chair of the ESV Bible Translation Oversight Committee and Executive Editor of the *ESV Study Bible*.

DANE C. ORTLUND (PhD, Wheaton College) serves as senior pastor of Naperville Presbyterian Church in Naperville, Illinois. He is an editor for the Knowing the Bible series and the Short Studies in Biblical Theology series, and is the author of several books, including *Gentle and Lowly: The Heart of Christ for Sinners and Sufferers*.

JONAH, MICAH, AND NAHUM

A 12-WEEK STUDY

Kristofer D. Holroyd

CROSSWAY®

WHEATON, ILLINOIS

Knowing the Bible: Jonah, Micah, and Nahum, A 12-Week Study

Copyright © 2018 by Crossway

Published by Crossway
        1300 Crescent Street
        Wheaton, Illinois 60187

Some content used in this study guide has been adapted from the *ESV Study Bible*, copyright © 2008 by Crossway, pages 1683–1718. Used by permission. All rights reserved.

Cover design: Simplicated Studio

First printing 2018

Printed in the United States of America

Unless otherwise indicated, Scripture quotations are from the ESV® Bible (The Holy Bible, English Standard Version®), copyright © 2001 by Crossway, a publishing ministry of Good News Publishers. Used by permission. All rights reserved.

The Scripture quotation marked NASB is from *The New American Standard Bible*®. Copyright © The Lockman Foundation 1960, 1962, 1963, 1968, 1971, 1972, 1973, 1975, 1977, 1995. Used by permission.

Trade paperback ISBN: 978-1-4335-5810-8
EPub ISBN: 978-1-4335-5813-9
PDF ISBN: 978-1-4335-5811-5
Mobipocket ISBN: 978-1-4335-5812-2

Crossway is a publishing ministry of Good News Publishers.

VP		33	32	31	30	29	28	27	26	25	24	23
14	13	12	11	10	9	8	7	6	5	4	3	2

TABLE OF CONTENTS

SERIES PREFACE

KNOWING THE BIBLE, as the series title indicates, was created to help readers know and understand the meaning, the message, and the God of the Bible. Each volume in the series consists of 12 units that progressively take the reader through a clear, concise study of one or more books of the Bible. In this way, any given volume can fruitfully be used in a 12-week format either in group study, such as in a church-based context, or in individual study. Of course, these 12 studies could be completed in fewer or more than 12 weeks, as convenient, depending on the context in which they are used.

Each study unit gives an overview of the text at hand before digging into it with a series of questions for reflection or discussion. The unit then concludes by highlighting the gospel of grace in each passage ("Gospel Glimpses"), identifying whole-Bible themes that occur in the passage ("Whole-Bible Connections"), and pinpointing Christian doctrines that are affirmed in the passage ("Theological Soundings").

The final component to each unit is a section for reflecting on personal and practical implications from the passage at hand. The layout provides space for recording responses to the questions proposed, and we think readers need to do this to get the full benefit of the exercise. The series also includes definitions of key words. These definitions are indicated by a note number in the text and are found at the end of each chapter.

Lastly, to help understand the Bible in this deeper way, we urge readers to use the ESV Bible and the *ESV Study Bible*, which are available in various print and digital formats, including online editions at esv.org. The *Knowing the Bible* series is also available online.

May the Lord greatly bless your study as you seek to know him through knowing his Word.

J. I. Packer

Lane T. Dennis

WEEK 1: OVERVIEW

▲

Jonah, Micah, and Nahum reveal God's directing of the nations for his purposes during the reemergence and ascendency of the Assyrian Empire. With messages of judgment against both Assyria and God's own people in Israel[1] and Judah, these prophets bring God's explanation of world events to his people as they endure both prosperity and punishment from the Lord.

Jonah begins our study with what seems to be a simple word of judgment against the Assyrian city of Nineveh. However, as we look more closely at the book, it becomes clear that this judgment is directed not just at Israel's enemies but actually against the people of Israel themselves. In their time of military expansion, wealth, and peace, Israel has become arrogant and self-focused, delighting in God's steadfast love toward them but wanting to keep that love for themselves.

Micah continues this judgment against Israel and Judah for their turning away from God, especially through their mistreatment of the weak and powerless among them. This wickedness, perpetrated and promoted by the leaders, prophets, and priests in Israel, would bring about the judgment of God at the hands of the Assyrians and, later, of the Babylonians. Nevertheless, God forgives sins and delights in restoring his people. Accordingly, Micah promises a coming Shepherd-King who will deliver God's people, restore them, and even take away those very things that led them astray.

Nahum concludes this time period with a condemning word against the

Assyrians. Although they experienced God's mercy and forgiveness because of their earlier repentance in the time of Jonah, they have once again exulted in violence and greed, and God's Word to them, like their treatment of others, is graphic and devastating. The city of Nineveh will be destroyed completely by the avenging warrior God of Israel. (For further background, see the *ESV Study Bible*, pages 1683–1718; available online at www.esv.org.)

Placing These Three Books in the Larger Story

These three short books together highlight the patience of God. Eager to forgive sins, God often allows the evil deeds of the wicked to pile up before he executes judgment, and this eagerness to forgive extends to all people everywhere, not just to Israel. In fact, Israel is supposed to be the herald of this great patient forgiveness, but, because of her own evil, God will bring judgment upon his people, too. These books, then, expose our sin, shame, and need for forgiveness and also point to the Great Shepherd who lays down his life for the sheep, making such forgiveness possible. Indeed, for those who put their trust in Jesus Christ, God will tread their iniquities underfoot and cast their sins into the depths of the sea.

Key Verses

"Who is a God like you, pardoning iniquity[2] and passing over transgression[3] for the remnant of his inheritance? He does not retain his anger forever, because he delights in steadfast love. He will again have compassion on us; he will tread our iniquities underfoot. You will cast all our sins into the depths of the sea." (Mic. 7:18–19)

Date and Historical Background

Around 780–745 BC the Assyrian Empire, which had largely ruled the ancient world for nearly a century, seemed to wane in power, and as a result of this temporarily waning influence, Jeroboam II continued his father's military expansion of Israel (2 Kings 14:23–28). Assyria's ebbing power, however, would not last long. Tiglath-pileser became king of the Assyrian Empire in 745 BC and quickly reestablished Assyrian dominance throughout the region. Like many of the Assyrian kings before him, Tiglath-pileser's reign was characterized by cruelty and destruction, especially upon those nations and peoples the Assyrians conquered. The northern kingdom of Israel experienced this cruelty, and in 722 BC it was devastated by the subsequent Assyrian king, Shalmaneser V, who ruled from 727–722 BC. Two kings later, Sennacherib (704–681 BC), made the prominent Assyrian city Nineveh the capital of the empire, enhancing the city and its defenses. However, less than one hundred years later, the city would be completely destroyed, and only a handful of years after that the empire itself would also be totally removed from history.

Into these world events, God sends his prophets with a message not just for Israel and Judah but also for Nineveh. The prophets of Jonah and Nahum sit as bookends surrounding Nineveh's reestablishment as a world power, with Jonah prophesying during the reign of Israel's king Jeroboam II (782–753 BC) and Nahum recording his oracles[4] and visions in Judah likely sometime between 660 and 630 BC. The ministry of Micah lasts a minimum of 20–25 years, though perhaps longer, as he prophesies during the reigns of Judah's kings Jotham, Ahaz, and Hezekiah, placing Micah's words sometime between 750 and 687 BC.

Outlines

Jonah

I. Jonah's Commissioning and Response (1:1–2:10)

  A. Jonah's commissioning and flight (1:1–3)

  B. Jonah and the pagan sailors (1:4–16)

  C. Jonah's grateful prayer (1:17–2:10)

II. Jonah's Recommissioning and Response (3:1–4:4)

  A. Jonah's recommissioning and compliance (3:1–3a)

  B. Jonah and the pagan Ninevites (3:3b–10)

  C. Jonah's angry prayer (4:1–4)

III. Jonah's Lesson about Compassion (4:5–11)

Micah

I. Superscription (1:1)

II. The Announcement of Judgment on Israel and Judah (1:2–2:13)

  A. God's punishment of Samaria and Judah (1:2–16)

    1. Judgment on Samaria (1:2–7)
    2. Judgment on Judah (1:8–16)

  B. Abuses and abusers of Yahweh's land (2:1–11)

    1. Indictment and future punishment (2:1–5)
    2. Rejection of the prophetic word (2:6–11)

  C. The divine promise to gather Jacob (2:12–13)

III. **The Present Injustice and the Future Prospect of Just Rule in Jerusalem (3:1–5:15)**

    A. Present leaders denounced (3:1–12)

        1. Judgment against the heads of Jacob (3:1–4)
        2. Judgment against the prophets (3:5–8)
        3. Judgment against the heads of Jacob (3:9–12)

    B. Jerusalem's restoration among the nations—promised (4:1–7)

        1. Nations approach Zion in peace (4:1–5)
        2. Divine promise to gather Zion (4:6–7)

    C. Jerusalem's restoration among the nations—accomplished (4:8–5:15)

        1. Restoration of Zion's dominion (4:8)
        2. Nations approach Zion for battle (4:9–13)
        3. The Shepherd-King arrives and the remnant is restored (5:1–15)

IV. **The Lord's Indictment and Restoration of His People (6:1–7:20)**

    A. Israel accused: covenant violation (6:1–8)

        1. The prophetic summons (6:1–2)
        2. Divine interrogation and saving acts (6:3–5)
        3. People's response and prophetic reply (6:6–8)

    B. Crisis in relationship (6:9–7:7)

        1. Divine indictment of treachery (6:9–12)
        2. Divine sentence for treachery (6:13–16)
        3. Consequence of disobedience: social upheaval (7:1–7)

    C. Zion's repentance and renewed faith in Yahweh's help (7:8–13)

    D. Restoration of the relationship between Israel and Yahweh (7:14–20)

Nahum

  I. Introduction (1:1)

 II. A Psalm Descriptively Praising the Lord (1:2–8)

    A. The Lord takes vengeance on his guilty adversaries (1:2–3a)

    B. The Lord rules creation in majesty, and no one can stand before his wrath (1:3b–6)

    C. The Lord delivers those who take refuge in him (1:7)

    D. The Lord destroys his adversaries (1:8)

III. The Lord's Coming Judgment on Nineveh and Deliverance of Judah (1:9–15)

    A. The destruction of wicked, plotting Nineveh (1:9–12a)

    B. Judah, having been afflicted by the Lord, is freed from Assyrian bondage (1:12b–13)

C. The termination of vile, idolatrous Nineveh (1:14)

D. Peace and deliverance for Judah (1:15)

IV. Focus on Nineveh: The Lord's Coming Judgment (2:1–13)

A. The beginning of the attack on Nineveh (2:1)

B. Reasons for judgment: the Assyrians' plundering of Judah, though Judah's restoration by God is planned (2:2)

C. Attacking soldiers and military action at Nineveh (2:3–5)

D. The fall and plundering of Nineveh (2:6–9)

E. A taunting song portraying Nineveh's destruction because of the city's lust for conquest (2:10–12)

F. The Lord speaks a word of judgment (2:13)

V. Again, Focus on Nineveh: More concerning the Lord's Coming Judgment (3:1–19)

A. Reasons for judgment: the violence, lying, and greed of Nineveh (3:1)

B. Military action at Nineveh and the ensuing slaughter of the Assyrians (3:2–3)

C. Reasons for judgment: the wickedness of Nineveh (3:4)

D. The Lord speaks a word of judgment (3:5–7)

E. Comparison with the conquest of Thebes (3:8–11)

F. A taunting song presenting Nineveh's inevitable destruction because of the city's incessant evil (3:12–19)

As You Get Started

Read each book—Jonah, Micah, and Nahum—straight through in one sitting. What are your first impressions? What stands out to you?

What words, phrases, and themes seem to span across these three books?

What questions do you have as you begin this study?

_____

_____

_____

_____

_____

As You Finish This Unit . . .

Take a few minutes to ask God to bless you with increased understanding and a transformed heart and life as you begin this study of Jonah, Micah, and Nahum.

Definitions

[1] **Israel** – Originally, another name given to Jacob (Gen. 32:28). Later applied to the nation formed by his descendants, then to the 10 northern tribes of that nation, who rejected the anointed king and formed their own nation. In the NT, the name is applied to the church as the spiritual descendants of Abraham (Gal. 6:16).

[2] **Iniquity** – Any violation of or failure to adhere to the commands of God, or the desire to do so.

[3] **Transgression** – A violation of a command or law.

[4] **Oracle** – From Latin "to speak." In the Bible, refers to a divine pronouncement delivered through a human agent.

Week 2: The Fear of the Lord

Jonah 1:1–2:10

The Place of the Passage

The book of Jonah opens with God calling the prophet to go and proclaim judgment against the enemies of Israel in the city of Nineveh; instead of following God's call, however, Jonah hops a boat going in the opposite direction from Nineveh. A violent storm threatens to overthrow the boat and take the life of everyone on it, but Jonah confesses his running from God and is thrown overboard, and the storm subsides. God sends a great fish to swallow Jonah, and while in the fish's belly the prophet offers up a prayer of thanksgiving for being rescued from death. After three days, the fish spits Jonah back onto dry land, preparing him for another opportunity to obey the Lord.

The Big Picture

Sometimes God uses terrifying situations so that we might learn to fear[1] the Lord rightly.

> **Reflection and Discussion**

Read through the complete passage for this study, Jonah 1:1–2:10. Then write your reflections on the following questions. (For further background, see the *ESV Study Bible*, pages 1687–1689; available online at www.esv.org.)

1. The Call and Flight of Jonah (1:1–3)

In the time of Jonah, the Assyrian Empire had not yet achieved the size and power that it would display several decades later. Nevertheless, the empire was dominant, and Assyrian kings were known for their violence and savagery, notably demonstrated in their torture of prisoners. Nineveh was one of Assyria's large and important cities, located more than 500 miles away from Jonah. What initial reasons might Jonah have for not wanting to go to Nineveh and "call out against it"?

Pronouncements of judgment in the Bible often serve as a warning and a call to repentance[2] for the people against whom judgment has been pronounced, and Jonah runs away from proclaiming judgment against Nineveh because he understands the message to be an opportunity for Nineveh to repent (see 4:2). Why do you think Jonah does not want the Ninevites to repent and turn to God?

Read Psalm 139:7–12. Twice in Jonah 1, the text says that Jonah is trying to get away "from the presence of the Lord." In light of Psalm 139, what do you think it means to flee from the presence of God? How do we try to do so today?

Where in your own life have you tried to get away from the presence of the Lord or to run from his Word, commands, or call?

2. The Fear of the Lord (1:4–2:10)

In 1:5 and 1:10, the sailors are afraid, and in 1:9 Jonah says that he "fears" the Lord. What is the difference between the sailors' fear and the fear of the Lord that Jonah says he has?

Once the sailors finally cast Jonah into the sea, the storm calms down and the sailors turn to the Lord. This turning to the Lord involves offering a sacrifice, a public expression of their worship, and it also involves their making certain vows, likely public expressions of their intention to continue to worship God. Notably, verse 16 describes this new relationship to the Lord in these words:

"[They] feared the LORD exceedingly." How does their new fear of the Lord contrast with Jonah's so-called fear of the Lord?

Read Jonah's prayer in 2:1–9 again, paying special attention to images he uses to describe his distress. How desperate is Jonah's situation? Note some of the ways in which he describes his desperation.

Both Jonah and the sailors are brought to places of distress, panic, and desperation before they learn to "fear the LORD." What does this teach us about God and the hard things we may endure in this life?

Although Jonah tried to flee from the Lord, God used the storm, the sailors, and the great fish to bring Jonah back to trusting in and following him. How, then, is the story of Jonah a comfort to God's people?

Read through the following three sections on *Gospel Glimpses, Whole-Bible Connections*, and *Theological Soundings*. Then take time to consider the *Personal Implications* these sections may have for you.

Gospel Glimpses

THREE DAYS. Jonah's near-death experience in the storm and sea, his "burial" in the fish, and his "resurrection" upon the dry land are used by Jesus to predict his own death, burial in the "heart of the earth," and eventual resurrection (Matt. 12:38–42). When Jesus in that passage says that "no sign will be given" to the people of his day "except the sign of the prophet Jonah," the sign—the miracle—to which Jesus points is not the appearance of the great fish but rather Jonah's rescue from death as a kind of resurrection. Jesus' actual resurrection from death would serve as the vindication of Jesus Christ as the Savior of sinners and as the verification of our very faith[3] (1 Cor. 15:12–34).

THE FEAR OF THE LORD. The fear of the Lord is not a fear of rejection or a cowering and trembling before a tyrant but rather a reverent awe of and devotion to God, along with a healthy fear of his fatherly displeasure and discipline (see Acts 5:5; 9:31; Phil. 2:12–13; 1 Pet. 1:17; 1 John 4:18). Such fear of the Lord is the foundation of knowledge (Prov. 1:7) and wisdom (Prov. 9:10) as we bow in humility before the Creator and Savior of the world.

Whole-Bible Connections

THE JUDGMENT OF STORMS. It was considered bad fortune to travel with prisoners or condemned persons in the ancient world, because it was believed that the gods would bring storms and calamity upon a ship that carried people of bad repute—as evidenced in the book of Jonah, as sailors cast lots in order to identify the person responsible for the supposed judgment from the gods. Furthermore, death from a shipwreck was often considered evidence of a person's guilt. In the New Testament, Luke would use these cultural beliefs to demonstrate the apostle Paul's innocence: though Paul was a prisoner on the way to trial in Rome, he survived unharmed both a storm and a shipwreck in Acts 27.

SLEEPING THROUGH THE STORM. Similar to Jonah, Jesus gets in a boat with his disciples[4] in order to cross the Sea of Galilee (Mark 4:35–41). Jesus, like Jonah, falls asleep and is deep in sleep during a violent storm. The disciples, like the sailors, fear for their lives and seek out their sleeping passenger to help them. Unlike Jonah, however, Jesus rises, rebukes the storm into silence, and then rebukes his disciples for their lack of faith. Undoubtedly told in such a way as to remind readers of the story of Jonah, this Gospel narrative relates how the disciples recognize Jesus' power to command the wind and sea, and, like the sailors when Jonah is cast into the sea, they turn and fear the Lord.

Theological Soundings

IRRESISTIBLE GOD. God's purposes will not be thwarted, nor, when "his hand is stretched out," can anyone turn it back (Isa. 14:27). This same sovereign power of God applies to his pursuit of his people: those whom God sets out to save and use for his purposes cannot resist him. This irresistibility applies to God's using those opposed to him—such as Pharaoh (Ex. 14:4), Joseph's brothers (Gen. 50:20), and even Jonah—to bring about his purposes. It applies especially to God's salvation of his people, ensuring that all those whom God sets out to save will indeed be saved by him (John 6:37).

LORD OF CREATION. The God who made heaven and earth rules over the forces of creation. He counts the stars and names them (Ps. 147:4); he measures the waters in his hand, marks the length and breadth of the heavens, counts the dust of the earth, and weighs the mountains in a balance and the hills in a pair of scales (Isa. 40:12; compare Job 38–39). He sends rain, wind, and lightning (Jer. 10:12–13; Job 5:10; Jonah 1:12), and he gives food to the birds and makes the flowers grow (Matt. 6:25–34). All things are in his hands, under his control, and directed by his will.

Personal Implications

Take time to reflect on the implications of Jonah 1:1–2:10 for your own life today. Consider what you have learned that might lead you to praise God, repent of sin, and trust in his gracious promises. Write down your reflections under the three headings we have considered and on the passage as a whole.

1. Gospel Glimpses

2. Whole-Bible Connections

3. Theological Soundings

4. Jonah 1:1–2:10

As You Finish This Unit . . .

Take a moment now to ask for the Lord's blessing and help as you continue in this study of Jonah, Micah, and Nahum. And take a moment also to look back through this unit of study, to reflect on some key things that the Lord may be teaching you.

Definitions

[1] **Fear** – Has both godly and ungodly meanings in the Bible, depending on the context. Fear of the Lord is a godly, wise fear that demonstrates awe and reverence for the all-powerful God (Prov. 1:7). Conversely, Jesus taught his disciples not to fear people or situations in a way that shows lack of trust in God's protection (Matt. 10:26–31).

[2] **Repentance** – A complete change of heart and mind regarding one's overall attitude toward God or one's individual actions. True regeneration and conversion is always accompanied by repentance.

[3] **Faith** – Trust in or reliance upon something or someone despite a lack of concrete proof. Salvation, which is purely a work of God's grace, can be received only through faith (Rom. 5:2; Eph. 2:8–9). The writer of Hebrews calls on believers to emulate those who lived godly lives by faith (Hebrews 11).

[4] **Disciple** – Any person who submits to the teachings of another. In the NT, refers to those who submitted themselves to the teaching of Jesus, especially those who traveled with him during his earthly ministry.

Week 3: Stubbornness and Repentance

Jonah 3:1–4:11

The Place of the Passage

Having been rescued from the storm and the fish because of God's steadfast love, Jonah responds with obedience to the word of the Lord and goes into Nineveh to preach the impending destruction of that great city. However, no sooner does Jonah begin preaching than the people of Nineveh believe God and cry out to him for mercy. Because of their repentance, God relents of the disaster he had planned. This mercy of God, however, infuriates Jonah. Accordingly, God provides Jonah an object lesson with a plant, a worm, and a scorching wind to teach him about compassion for others.

The Big Picture

God's steadfast love toward us should fill our hearts with that same love toward others.

> ## Reflection and Discussion

Read through the complete passage for this study, Jonah 3:1–4:11. Then write your reflections on the following questions. (For further background, see the *ESV Study Bible*, pages 1689–1691; available online at www.esv.org.)

1. The Repentance of Nineveh (3:1–10)

Jonah 3:3 notes that Jonah finally obeys the word of the Lord, going to Nineveh to pronounce God's judgment upon the city. How is Jonah's response to this second call of God related to what Jonah experienced through the storm and the fish in chapter 1? In other words, why does Jonah obey God this time instead of running away?

We tend to think of "prophecy" simply as something that predicts the future. However, biblical prophecy is about much more than foretelling upcoming events; it is primarily concerned with the moral formation of God's people through the proclamation of God's Word. Read Jeremiah 18:1–11. Why does God tell the Ninevites that they will be destroyed in 40 days?

Although the city of Nineveh is described as being "three days' journey in breadth," the text notes that Jonah goes only a day's journey. This shortened trip seems to be the result of the rapidity with which the Ninevites respond to Jonah's message; their repentance is immediate, perhaps spreading through the city before Jonah himself could spread the message (see the notes on verses

5 and 7–8 in the *ESV Study Bible*). What does this immediate response from the Ninevites tell us about their faith? (See also Matt. 19:16–22; Acts 2:37; 8:36.)

2. The Stubbornness of Jonah (4:1–11)

Jonah is angry over God's relenting of the disaster he announced against Nineveh. In fact, the Hebrew text of 4:1 says that, to Jonah, this relenting was "exceedingly evil" (see ESV footnote). Why is Jonah so angry?

Jonah's anger actually seems to be directed against God's own character (v. 2; see also the corresponding notes in the *ESV Study Bible*). How is Jonah's anger unjust, or at least inconsistent with his own experience of God's character? How is that inconsistency demonstrated in the very words Jonah uses for his complaint?

Four times in the book of Jonah, God "appoints" something (1:17; 4:6, 7, 8). What does this demonstration of God's appointing teach us about him? How is this relevant to the message of the book of Jonah?

Read Genesis 18:16–33. Ancient Jewish interpreters of Genesis often herald Abraham's intercession for Sodom as even nobler than his obedience to God when asked to sacrifice his only son (Genesis 22). How does Abraham's concern for the city of Sodom, which did not have even 10 righteous persons within it, contrast with Jonah's concern for Nineveh, filled with those "who do not know their right hand from their left" (Jonah 4:11)? How does the story of Abraham's concern for Sodom impact our understanding of the book of Jonah?

Why does God include "much cattle" in his appeal to Jonah in 4:11? How is this a further indictment against Jonah?

Three times in the book of Jonah, "pagans"[1] express care for those who are perishing (1:6, 14; 3:9). However, Jonah, the representative of God's people, seems to care only for himself and the "perishing" of a plant from which he personally benefits (4:10). Do you today see nonbelievers leading in the care for others who may be perishing rather than the church of Jesus Christ leading in that care? Where has the church become more concerned over her own well-being than over the well-being of others?

The concluding of Jonah with an open-ended question invites us to view ourselves as addressees of the same question. Indeed, it is easy to assume that God is on our side—with "us" and opposed to "them." This assumption is often made in war, politics, and even interpersonal conflicts. Where, then, are we like Jonah?

Where do we expect God to take our side and to be against our "enemies" or opponents? Where are we offended or even angry at God's character because God's compassion is not limited to "us" but available also to "them"?

Read through the following three sections on *Gospel Glimpses*, *Whole-Bible Connections*, and *Theological Soundings*. Then take time to consider the *Personal Implications* these sections may have for you.

Gospel Glimpses

RESULTS OF REPENTANCE. When people turn away from sin and toward God, with grief over their sins (Jonah 3:5) and an earnest desire for mercy and forgiveness (v. 9), God forgives their sins and restores the penitent to right relationship with him. Indeed, this forgiveness of sins as a result of repentance is rooted in the very character of God, for, as Jonah notes, God is gracious, "merciful, slow to anger and abounding in steadfast love" (4:2).

THE FRUIT OF FAITH. Jonah's renewed obedience is a direct result of his experience of the salvation of God, because obedience is the natural fruit of faith. Jesus says, "If you love me, you will keep my commandments" (John 14:15); the apostle Paul reminds us that our lives are sacrifices of thanksgiving for what God has done for us (Rom. 12:1–2); and James calls us to demonstrate our faith by good works (James 2:14–26). Experiencing God's mercy and grace[2] in salvation should lead us to respond with thankful obedience that demonstrates our grateful hearts.

Whole-Bible Connections

FOR THE NATIONS. One of the purposes of the book of Jonah is to teach God's people that his salvation is for people from every nation. The Old Testament people of God, like Jonah, struggled to believe God could show compassion and mercy to those not of ethnic Israel, and the church in the New Testament struggled to receive Christians who were not of Jewish background. Accordingly, in some ways the book of Acts functions as a New Testament Jonah, as God teaches his people that the gospel is for people of every tongue, tribe, and nation through the progressive outpouring of the Holy Spirit[3] to different ethnic groups (see Acts 10:44–48 and the corresponding notes in the *ESV Study Bible*).

A DETERMINED GOD. God's plan from the beginning of Scripture was to bring his salvation to all nations (Gen. 12:1–3), and the book of Jonah reminds us of God's determination to do just that: his message of salvation will go to all the ends of the earth. In the New Testament, we see that same determination in the commission Jesus gives to his disciples after his resurrection (Matt. 28:19–20) and in God's protection of the apostle Paul in the book of Acts, ensuring that the gospel reaches Rome (Acts 27–28).

Theological Soundings

CONDITIONAL PROPHECY. Much of the prophecy in the Old Testament, particularly pronouncements of judgment or blessing, was conditional. Instead of being definitive statements of guaranteed future events, they were, rather, warnings of what would happen if the recipients did not turn back to the Lord, or promises of blessing if they continued in faithfulness to the Lord. Such prophecies, as conditional warnings and promises rather than definitive predictions, reveal that God is more concerned with our belief and repentance than he is in simply displaying his knowledge of the future. This is seen clearly in his "relenting" of disaster on Nineveh because of the city's repentance.

GOD'S RELENTING. Often in the Bible, God is said to relent of the disaster he had spoken against a certain group or nation (see Ex. 32:14; Jer. 26:3; Jonah 3:10). There is a close connection between human actions and God's response, and, indeed, from a human perspective it appears that God responds or reacts to human activity. However, from an eternal perspective, it is clear that God ordains both the means and the end result. In other words, he plans both the end result (relenting from disaster) and the means by which that relenting occurs (the warning of judgment and the repentance of the people). He sovereignly reigns over every aspect of our lives and salvation, including, for example, by proclaiming a message of disaster, enabling the repentance of his people, and blessing them by not bringing about the forewarned disaster.

Personal Implications

Take time to reflect on the implications of Jonah 3:1–4:11 for your own life today. Consider what you have learned that might lead you to praise God, repent of sin, and trust in his gracious promises. Write down your reflections under the three headings we have considered and on the passage as a whole.

1. Gospel Glimpses

2. Whole-Bible Connections

3. Theological Soundings

4. Jonah 3:1–4:11

As You Finish This Unit . . .

Take a moment now to ask for the Lord's blessing and help as you continue in this study of Jonah, Micah, and Nahum. And take a moment also to look back through this unit of study, to reflect on some key things that the Lord may be teaching you.

Definitions

[1] **Paganism** – Any belief system that does not acknowledge the God of the Bible as the one true God. Atheism, polytheism, pantheism, animism, and humanism, as well as numerous other religious systems, can all be classified as forms of paganism.

[2] **Grace** – Unmerited favor, especially the free gift of salvation that God gives to believers through faith in Jesus Christ.

[3] **Holy Spirit** – One of the persons of the Trinity, and thus fully God. The Bible mentions several roles of the Holy Spirit, including convicting people of sin, bringing them to conversion, indwelling them, empowering them to live in righteousness and faithfulness, supporting them in times of trial, and enabling them to understand the Scriptures. The Holy Spirit inspired the writers of Scripture, guiding them to record the very words of God. The Holy Spirit was especially active in Jesus' life and ministry on earth (e.g., Luke 3:22).

Week 4: The Lord of Creation against His People

Micah 1:1–16

▲

The Place of the Passage

The book of Micah opens with God summoning the people of the earth to come and witness his judgment against Israel. Both northern Israel, represented by the city of Samaria, and the southern kingdom of Judah, represented by the city of Jerusalem, are under divine condemnation. The first half of the first chapter establishes God's authority and power through the disruption of creation itself at his coming, and then the prophet announces the unmaking of Samaria as the city is returned to its pre-inhabited state. The second half of the chapter begins the judgment against Judah through a series of wordplays using the city names of some of the prominent communities of Judah.

The Big Picture

The Lord Almighty, before whom creation itself quakes, will come to judge his people for their sin.

Reflection and Discussion

Read through the complete passage for this study, Micah 1:1–16. Then write your reflections on the following questions. (For further background, see the *ESV Study Bible*, pages 1696–1698; available online at www.esv.org.)

1. Judgment against Samaria (1:1–7)

In Leviticus 18:24–30, the Lord explains to Israel that the land of Canaan, of which they were about to take possession, "vomited out its inhabitants" because the Canaanites had become unclean[1] and had defiled the land. That judgment against the Canaanites stood as an example to Israel of what would happen to them if they took up the practices of the Canaanites and also became unclean. As we begin the book of Micah, we see God calling all the inhabits of the earth to come and witness his judgment against his own people, Israel. In light of Leviticus 18:24–30, why does God summon the nations to witness the judgment against Israel?

In Micah 1:4, the coming of the Lord in judgment is accompanied by a disturbing of creation, in language that perhaps intentionally seems to reverse God's act of creating the earth. How does such cosmic disturbance prepare the way for a word of judgment?

Just as creation seems to be undone by the coming of the Lord in judgment, Samaria will be undone. Note the ways in which the creation of Samaria is reversed. How does Samaria return to its preexistent state (vv. 5–6)?

The wealth of Samaria appears to have come, in part, from the revenue of cultic prostitution. Idols[2] were made from the gold and silver used to pay for prostitutes. Additionally, exploitation of the weak and powerless and the conquest of neighboring nations enabled Israel to purchase or craft the most expensive idols. Verse 7 notes that the impending punishment would see the Assyrian army using the precious metals taken from Samaria to increase the extravagance of their own cultic centers. How is this an appropriate punishment for the sin of Samaria?

----

2. Judgment against Judah (1:8–16)

Each of the cities listed in verses 10–15 was within a few miles of Micah's hometown of Moresheth Gath, and may even have been visible from there. The judgment against Judah uses this rapid succession of city names, in addition to word play with their names, to increase the dramatic effect of that judgment. Using the notes in the *ESV Study Bible*, record what you learn about Judah's judgment from each of the city names below and its corresponding wordplay:

Beth-le-aphrah

Shaphir

_____

_____

_____

_____

Zaanan

_____

_____

_____

_____

Beth-ezel

_____

_____

_____

_____

Maroth

_____

_____

_____

_____

Lachish

_____

_____

_____

_____

Moresheth-gath

_____

_____

_____

_____

Achzib

Mareshah

Two cities *not* listed above, the first and last mentioned in these verses, frame the judgment by referencing times of sorrow and distress in the life of King David. The first, Gath (v. 10a), recalls David's mourning over the death of King Saul in 2 Samuel 1:20, and the last, Adullam (v. 15b), recalls David's pre-king days of fleeing for his life in the wilderness, when he was forced to hide in caves such as those at Adullam (1 Sam. 22:1; 2 Sam. 23:13). How do these allusions to the life of David further illuminate the coming judgment against Judah?

Read through the following three sections on *Gospel Glimpses*, *Whole-Bible Connections*, and *Theological Soundings*. Then take time to consider the *Personal Implications* these sections may have for you.

Gospel Glimpses

PARADIGMATIC JUDGMENT. All throughout the Bible, we see God's judgment upon the people of earth; this includes judgment against the wicked in general (e.g., Sodom in Gen. 19:23–29), against wicked individuals (e.g., Jezebel in 2 Kings 9:30–37), against the nations in general (e.g., Joel 3:9–12), against particular nations (e.g., Jeremiah 46–51), against God's people in general (e.g., Micah 1), and against individuals within God's people (e.g., David's census in 2 Samuel 24). These judgments of God throughout Scripture serve as a reminder that one day everyone will stand before God and receive from him according to what they have done, whether good or evil (2 Cor. 5:10; Rev. 22:12).

LEX TALIONIS. The law of retaliation, or *lex talionis*, was a means of punishment given to the civil authorities in the Old Testament that punished an offender by inflicting the same harm he had inflicted on another. Not a means for personal revenge, this law of paying "an eye for an eye" was instead a means of providing justice, purging evil, and even protecting perpetrators from excessive or inappropriate punishment. Such precise justice helps us see the justice of God and the need for repayment when we wrong others. Furthermore, it helps us understand the need for the death of Jesus, because our sins must be paid for, and God's justice must be satisfied.

Whole-Bible Connections

OBJECT LESSONS. In Micah 1:8–9, the prophet's going around stripped and naked certainly expresses his mourning over the judgment coming upon Israel, but it also serves as a visual sign of warning to God's people, who would be stripped of all they had and carried off into exile.[3] The Bible is full of such symbolic actions from the prophets, beginning with Moses' removing his shoes in the presence of God (Ex. 3:5) and including such acts as walking naked and barefoot for three years (Isaiah 20), smashing a flask (Jeremiah 19), eating a scroll (Ezek. 3:2–3), and lying on one side for 390 days and for 40 days on the other (Ezek. 4:4–8). Such actions serve to communicate God's truths in dramatic and memorable ways.

JACKALS AND OSTRICHES. The Bible often uses animals such as jackals and ostriches to depict the desolation that would come with the judgment of God (Isa. 34:13; Jer. 50:39). Known as creatures of the night and of the desert, jackals and ostriches were also known for their howling, making them an especially apt picture of the despair of total judgment (Mic. 1:8), and ostriches in particular were known for their vicious treatment of their own young, making them an illustration of the savagery to which people would descend in such desperate times (Job 39:13–18; Lam. 4:3).

TEMPLE PROSTITUTES. The nations surrounding Israel in the ancient world believed that the fertility of the world was brought forth through the sexual union of a god and a goddess, and such union, they believed, could be conjured or encouraged by the practice of "sacred" prostitution. Through the physical intimacy of a person and a temple prostitute, the gods would be encouraged to practice their intimacy, the land would once again receive rain and produce crops, and the herds and children of the worshipers would likewise multiply.

Theological Soundings

THE LAND. In many ways, the Old Testament is focused on humanity's relationship to God, to each other, and to the earth, represented by the Promised Land. Leviticus 18:24–30 teaches that there is a relationship between us and the earth and that the earth itself is impacted by our actions, as Micah also demonstrates. This relationship was broken from early in our history when the first man and first woman sinned against God; because of their sin, the earth itself was cursed with thorns and thistles (Gen. 3:17–19). Accordingly, the earth eagerly awaits the return of King Jesus and the restoration of all things, groaning in anticipation of its own release from the curse and the effects of our sin (Rom. 8:18–22).

Personal Implications

Take time to reflect on the implications of Micah 1:1–16 for your own life today. Consider what you have learned that might lead you to praise God, repent of sin, and trust in his gracious promises. Write down your reflections under the three headings we have considered and on the passage as a whole.

1. Gospel Glimpses

2. Whole-Bible Connections

3. Theological Soundings

4. Micah 1:1–16

> ## As You Finish This Unit . . .

Take a moment now to ask for the Lord's blessing and help as you continue in this study of Jonah, Micah, and Nahum. And take a moment also to look back through this unit of study, to reflect on some key things that the Lord may be teaching you.

Definitions

[1] **Clean/unclean** – The ceremonial, spiritual, or moral state of a person or object, affected by a variety of factors. The terms are primarily related to the concept of holiness and have little to do with actual physical cleanliness. The Mosaic law declared certain foods and animals unclean, and a person became unclean if he or she came in contact with certain substances or objects, such as a dead body. Jesus declared all food clean (Mark 7:19), and Peter's vision in Acts 10 shows that no person is ceremonially unclean simply because he or she is a Gentile.

[2] **Idolatry** – In the Bible, usually refers to the worship of a physical object. Paul's comments in Colossians 3:5, however, suggest that idolatry can include covetousness, since it is essentially equivalent to worshiping material things.

[3] **Exile** – Several relocations of large groups of Israelites/Jews have occurred throughout history, but "the exile" typically refers to the Babylonian exile, that is, Nebuchadnezzar's relocation of residents of the southern kingdom of Judah to Babylon in 586 BC. (Residents of the northern kingdom of Israel had been resettled by Assyria in 722 BC.) After Babylon came under Persian rule, several waves of Jewish exiles returned and repopulated Judah.

WEEK 5: A FAILURE OF LEADERSHIP

Micah 2:1–3:12

▲

Micah continues his pronouncement of judgment against Israel with a rebuke of her leaders. These leaders have used their power, influence, and money to take advantage of the weak and powerless and to suppress the Word of God. Even the prophets, who were to be the voice of God to his people, have become corrupt and proclaim only what those who pay them want to hear. Therefore, because of this failure of leadership, the land will become a desolation, a heap of ruins. Yet there is hope! A Shepherd-King is promised who will regather God's people and lead them out of their captivity.

The Big Picture

Although the leaders of Israel have brought the judgment of God upon the nation, a Shepherd-King will one day restore the remnant of God's people.

Reflection and Discussion

Read through the complete passage for this study, Micah 2:1–3:12. Then write your reflections on the following questions. (For further background, see the *ESV Study Bible*, pages 1698–1701; available online at www.esv.org.)

1. Abusing God's Word (2:1–11; 3:1–8)

Read 1 Kings 21:1–16. Even though the events of 1 Kings 21 occurred many years before the ministry of Micah, they paint a picture of the kinds of abuses taking place among the powerful in Micah's day. These abuses are described using the image of cannibalism at the beginning of Micah 3. Why are such abuses so heinous to God (2:1–2)?

The land in Israel was divided among the 12 tribes, and within each tribe it was allocated to each family in the tribe. The land was passed down from generation to generation and remained in the family. A family could find itself in hard times, during which the family could sell its land, and sell themselves as servants, to another Israelite family. However, the year of Jubilee, which occurred every fiftieth year, reset the land allocations so that each family once again possessed its ancestral inheritance (Lev. 25:8–22). How does this background inform your understanding of the punishment being brought upon those oppressing the people (Mic. 2:4–5)?

How are the people responding to or abusing the Word of God (2:6, 11; 3:5, 11)?

In Hebrew, the phrase "when they have something to eat" (3:5) is literally "who bite with their teeth." This phrase uses a word that occurs 11 other times in the Old Testament, with 10 of those 11 times relating to snakes (e.g., the fiery serpents biting the people in Num. 21:6). In the one other occurrence of the word, it refers to lending money with interest; high interest rates were one more means of oppressing those who fell on hard times (Deut. 23:19–20). How does this expression help paint a picture of the destruction these prophets' false proclamations were bringing upon God's people?

What are the specific punishments God will bring upon the people for their rejection of his Word (Mic. 3:4–7)?

Read Proverbs 21:10–13 and the corresponding notes in the *ESV Study Bible*. Why will God not answer the cries of the people in Micah 3:4–7? See also Matthew 25:31–46.

2. A Contrast of Leaders (2:12–13; 3:9–12)

Micah lays the blame for the coming destruction of Israel clearly at the feet of the leaders: heads, priests,[1] and prophets. Without equivocation, he boldly proclaims that disaster is coming "because of you" (3:12; compare 2:3). Although Israel is certainly in a unique situation as a nation due her particular national relationship to God, it remains nevertheless true for Israel that, as the king goes, so goes the nation. How, then, does this add weight to the apostle Paul's command that we are to pray for all people, especially "for kings and all who are in high positions" (1 Tim. 2:1–2)?

Despite the judgment on Israel, especially Israel's leaders, these chapters are not without hope. What are the two images used in Micah 2:12–13, and how do they offer hope to Israel?

How is the leadership of the promised Shepherd-King different from that which the people are currently experiencing?

Read through the following three sections on *Gospel Glimpses*, *Whole-Bible Connections*, and *Theological Soundings*. Then take time to consider the *Personal Implications* these sections may have for you.

Gospel Glimpses

INHERITANCE. The Israelite ancestral land passed down from generation to generation was part of the promised inheritance for God's people through their relationship with him. Even if the people fell onto hard times and had to sell either their inheritance or themselves as servants, the law of Jubilee promised a day when their inheritance would once again be returned to their family (see a negative example of this in Micah 2:4–5). This ancestral inheritance points to the eternal inheritance we have in Jesus Christ: those who put their faith in Jesus become inheritors of their heavenly Father and will one day, at the return of Christ, possess that inheritance (Heb. 9:15; Rom. 8:17; Eph. 3:6).

THE SHEPHERD-KING. Micah promises a future deliverer who will gather God's people as a shepherd gathers his flock but will also fight for them and lead them as their King. Such imagery, reminiscent of King David, a shepherd who eventually became king (1 Sam. 16:11–13; 2 Sam. 2:1–4), anticipates a coming King like David who will once again gather God's people, fight for them against their enemies, deliver them from bondage, bring about lasting peace, and rule over them with justice. With echoes of Israel's deliverance out of Egypt (Ex. 13:21; Deut. 1:30–33), Micah proclaims that the Lord himself will be that Shepherd-King. Of course, Micah's original audience would likely hear such a promise in terms of God's Spirit being with a human king, as the Spirit was with David. However, God's plans were much greater, as it was indeed God Himself, the Lord made flesh,[2] who would rescue his people through his own life, death, and resurrection.

Whole-Bible Connections

FALSE PROPHETS. Throughout the history of Israel, God's true prophets were always contending against false prophets (e.g., Amos vs. Amaziah in Amos 7:10–17; Jeremiah vs. Hananiah in Jeremiah 28). These false prophets, motivated perhaps by a desire for money, acceptance, or power, often proclaimed peace, prosperity, and victory for Israel without having actually heard any such promise from the Lord. The Lord condemns such false prophets in the strongest language (Jer. 23:9–40; Ezekiel 13; Mic. 3:5–8).

REMNANT. God's judgment often seems to threaten the total annihilation of humanity, as in the days of Noah (Genesis 6); and sometimes the spread of wickedness seems to threaten total annihilation of God's people, as in the days of Elijah (1 Kings 19). In both cases, however, God preserved for himself a remnant, a small group of those faithful to him, through whom he preserved the reputation and glory of his name. In the days of Noah, God preserved the remnant of Noah and his family; in the days of Elijah, God preserved 7,000 in Israel who had not worshiped the false god Baal. Throughout the struggles of Israel in the Old Testament, God always preserved a remnant of his people, a small group of those called by God and faithful to him (e.g., Isa. 10:20–23; Mic. 2:12–13). Similarly today, despite judgment on the earth or the apparent expansion of wickedness to the detriment of the church, God preserves his people as a remnant among all people on earth, protecting the reputation and glory of his name through that remnant.

Theological Soundings

THE SPIRIT OF PROPHECY. Micah notes that which distinguishes him from the false prophets: he is filled with the Spirit of the Lord (3:8). The Holy Spirit inspired the prophets of old for the proclamation of God's Word and for the recording of that Word. For this reason, God often accompanied his Word with either miracles[3] or the fulfillment of short-term predictions in order to give visible, audible attestations of his approval upon those he appointed to proclaim his Word. For example, Moses received the law amid smoke, fire, and thunder (Exodus 19); and the prophet who confronted Jeroboam and predicted the rise of Josiah a few hundred years later accompanied that word with both a miracle (the shriveling of Jeroboam's hand) and the short-term fulfilled prophecy of the breaking down of the altar (1 Kings 13:1–10). Even the disciples of Jesus received such authenticating signs, as they were God's messengers for the giving of the New Testament (e.g., Acts 9:36–43; 19:11–20). These miracles or short-term fulfilled predictions authenticated the messengers as true prophets of the Lord and give us confidence in knowing that the text we have today is truly the Word of God.

TRUE AND UNDEFILED RELIGION. The Bible makes clear that God cares for the orphan, the widow, the sojourner, the alien, the weak, and the impoverished. God is described as a Father to the fatherless and a protector of widows (Pss. 68:5; 146:9), and he commands his people to care for these groups of people who are close to his heart and are the most likely to be abused or taken advantage of by society and those in power (Ps. 82:3; Isa. 58:6–12; Jer. 7:6; 22:1–5). Regarding this care for the orphan, the widow, and the oppressed, James refers to it as religion "that is pure and undefiled before God" (James 1:27).

Personal Implications

Take time to reflect on the implications of Micah 2:1–3:12 for your own life today. Consider what you have learned that might lead you to praise God, repent of sin,

and trust in his gracious promises. Write down your reflections under the three headings we have considered and on the passage as a whole.

1. Gospel Glimpses

2. Whole-Bible Connections

3. Theological Soundings

4. Micah 2:1–3:12

As You Finish This Unit . . .

Take a moment now to ask for the Lord's blessing and help as you continue in this study of Jonah, Micah, and Nahum. And take a moment also to look back through this unit of study, to reflect on some key things that the Lord may be teaching you.

Definitions

[1] **Priest** – In OT Israel, the priest represented the people before God, and he represented God before the people. Only those descended from Aaron could be priests. Their prescribed duties also included inspecting and receiving sacrifices from the people and overseeing the daily activities and maintenance of the tabernacle or temple.

[2] **Flesh** – Depending on the immediate context, either skin (Lev. 4:11), a living being (Gen. 6:13), or sinful human nature (Rom. 8:3). When referring to Jesus' becoming flesh, it means his becoming human with both skin and a human—though not sinful—nature.

[3] **Miracle** – A special act of God that goes beyond natural means, thus demonstrating God's power.

WEEK 6: HE SHALL
BE THEIR PEACE

Micah 4:1–5:15

▲

The Place of the Passage

After grave condemnations of Israel's leaders, Micah pronounces Israel's future: Assyria and Babylon will come in judgment against God's people, taking them into exile. Nevertheless, like a woman enduring the pains of labor, after a time a Savior will be born. Continuing the Shepherd-King imagery from chapter 2, Micah declares that this Savior will regather those who have been driven away and will usher in a reign of peace.[1] This King, moreover, will rid the people even of those very things that have led them away from the Lord, and the Lord God will be exalted in the eyes of all the nations.

The Big Picture

The suffering and pain of God's people will give way to the victory and peace of their Shepherd-King.

Reflection and Discussion

Read through the complete passage for this study, Micah 4:1–5:15. Then write your reflections on the following questions. (For further background, see the *ESV Study Bible*, pages 1701–1704; available online at www.esv.org.)

1. Lasting Peace (4:1–13)

The "mountain of the house of the LORD" refers to the Temple Mount in Jerusalem, which Micah notes will become "plowed as a field" and will be destroyed into "a heap of ruins" (3:12). But God will rebuild his holy city and his temple, lifting them to the highest mountain. In the ancient world, the gods were believed to live on the mountains, so if the Lord is exalted on the highest mountain, what does that say about him to relation to the other so-called gods? How does this inform our understanding of why the nations will then flow to him (4:1)?

The knowledge of God comes from "the house of the God of Jacob," "out of Zion," and "from Jerusalem" (4:2). What does this teach us about the mission and purpose of Israel, especially with regard to the nations (compare Gen. 12:1–3; Isa. 42:5–9)?

Micah ministers during a time in which the balance of power in the world is shifting between Egypt, Assyria, and Babylon. Wars constantly rage, and the rest of the Middle East is constantly being traded between these powers through military conquest. What, then, is the hope Micah offers in 4:3–4?

Today, as wars still rage around the globe and the threat of terrorist attacks looms over our cities, we still need the hope offered by Micah. How would you translate the images of Micah 4:3–4 into an image for today?

Review the map in the introduction to Micah (page 1695 of the *ESV Study Bible*) and note the size of the Assyrian territory compared to the size of Israel. Micah 4 draws attention to the weakness of Israel through a series of images depicting the lame (vv. 6–7), kinglessness (v. 9), and a woman in labor (vv. 9–10). How do these images contrast with and prepare for the hope offered in verses 11–13? How are these new images pictures of strength?

2. Lasting Rule (5:1–15)

What do we learn of the coming Messiah[2] from Micah 5:1–6?

How should this impact your understanding of the person and work of Jesus Christ?

In 5:10–15, the Lord variously cuts off, destroys, throws down, and roots out. How are these destructive acts of the coming Messiah a means of salvation for his people? How is this destruction beneficial?

How does this destruction of the causes of sin among God's people inform our reading of the promise in Revelation 21:4 that, on the last day, God "will wipe away every tear from their eyes, and death shall be no more, neither shall there be mourning, nor crying, nor pain anymore, for the former things have passed away"?

God gives Israel this promise of future deliverance: it will be a day when his people will be rescued, the nations shall come to learn from his people, God's people will rule over the nations, and there will be lasting peace. Notice that this promise is given *before* Israel goes into captivity or exile (Mic. 4:10; 5:1, 3, 5). How does having this promise of future deliverance prepare the people for their impending time of suffering? How should these promises have sustained them during that suffering?

A day is coming when King Jesus will return and rule over the nations, bringing a final end to his and our enemies and ushering in his kingdom of eternal peace. How should God's promise of our future deliverance at the return of Christ sustain us through times of suffering?

Read through the following three sections on *Gospel Glimpses*, *Whole-Bible Connections*, and *Theological Soundings*. Then take time to consider the *Personal Implications* these sections may have for you.

Gospel Glimpses

PROMISING SALVATION. In our text this week, God promises salvation for his people even before they have suffered. Prior to Assyria's devastating the northern kingdom of Israel and prior to Babylon's carrying the southern kingdom of Judah into exile, God already promises that he will rescue Israel (Mic. 4:10), give them victory over their enemies (4:11–13), bring them back home (5:3), and deliver them (5:6). God similarly promises salvation from Babylon through Jeremiah, informing the people that their captivity will last 70 years (Jer. 29:10). Since defeat at the hands of Assyria and Babylon is discipline for Israel's sin, such promises remind God's people that such discipline has an end; and for those innocent of the crimes for which Israel's leaders are condemned, such promises grant hope for the end of their suffering.

SEASONAL PICTURES. The Bible frequently uses images from creation to illustrate God's actions. For example, Isaiah 1:18 tells us that "though [our] sins are like scarlet," God washes them "as white as snow"; Hosea 6:1–3 reminds us that healing from the Lord and new life come like "the spring rains that water the earth"; and the fall harvest in Micah 4:12–13 is a picture of God's coming judgment, when he will reap the nations. Such pictures give us regular reminders of the actions and promises of God, so that as the seasons change and we witness the patterns of creation, we will meditate on the work of the Lord.

Whole-Bible Connections

LATTER DAYS. The term "latter days" refers to an unspecified time in the future, typically a terminus of some sort. For example, the prophet Balaam uses the expression to refer to Israel's prosperity and military might under King David, during which Israel will conquer Moab (Num. 24:14); Daniel uses the term to describe the ongoing future as kingdoms rise and fall (Dan. 2:28); and Deuteronomy 4:30 uses the term to refer to a possible time in which, if the people end up in exile, they will return to the Lord and be brought back to the land. Indeed, this last use of the expression is perhaps the most prominent way it is used in the prophets (compare Isa. 2:2; Hos. 3:5; Mic. 4:1), and it combines the nearer future hope of deliverance from exile and return to the land with the more distant future hope of the Messianic age, in which the future King will rule for all eternity.

THE MISSION OF ISRAEL. The land of Canaan, sometimes called the "sacred bridge," was the only way to travel between Egypt and Mesopotamia in the ancient world. With two major roadways through the land, one following the coast of the Mediterranean Sea and the other passing just east of the Jordan River, travelers could avoid the treacherous trek through the Arabian Desert. This ideal location put Israel at the crossroads of the major kingdoms of that time. Accordingly, God's mission for Israel was *centripetal* in nature; that is, God brought the nations to Israel, where they would, ideally, see the people of Israel, learn of their God, and join together with Israel in worshiping the one true God. After the resurrection and ascension[3] of Jesus, the mission of the church transitioned to a more *centrifugal* model, in which God's people went out into all the nations instead of the nations coming to Israel (Matt. 28:19; Acts 1:8).

Theological Soundings

LORD OF HOSTS. The title "LORD of Hosts" (Mic. 4:4) refers to God's might and power by using the image of a commander who leads the armies, or "hosts," of heaven. In 2 Kings 6:17, the prophet Elisha prays for his servant to be able to see the armies of the Lord encamped around them, and Jesus tells his disciples and those gathered to arrest him that he simply need ask his Father and "more than twelve legions of angels" would be sent to fight for him (Matt. 26:53). The title "LORD of Hosts" describes our God as one who fights for his people (Deut. 1:30–31), and the title anticipates the last day, on which the Lord Jesus Christ will return with his armies of heaven to establish his reign fully and finally as King of kings and Lord of lords (Rev. 19:11–16).

INTERNAL AFFIRMATION. One of the affirmations of the Bible's authority as God's Word is the various human authors' treatment of other Bible texts. For example, the text of Micah 4:1–3 appears with nearly the same wording in Isaiah 2:2–4. Regardless of whether Micah or Isaiah borrowed from the other or the two used a common source, this use of the same text points to their mutual view of the text as coming from the Holy Spirit. This is seen also in the New Testament, as Peter equates the writings of Paul with "the other Scriptures" (2 Pet. 3:15–16). Such internal affirmations, of course, include the New Testament's references to the Old Testament with such introductions as "the Holy Spirit says" (e.g., Heb. 3:7; 10:15).

Personal Implications

Take time to reflect on the implications of Micah 4:1–5:15 for your own life today. Consider what you have learned that might lead you to praise God, repent of sin, and trust in his gracious promises. Write down your reflections under the three headings we have considered and on the passage as a whole.

1. Gospel Glimpses

2. Whole-Bible Connections

3. Theological Soundings

4. Micah 4:1–5:15

> ### As You Finish This Unit . . .

Take a moment now to ask for the Lord's blessing and help as you continue in this study of Jonah, Micah, and Nahum. And take a moment also to look back through this unit of study, to reflect on some key things that the Lord may be teaching you.

Definitions

[1] **Peace** – In modern use, the absence of tension or conflict. In biblical use, a condition of well-being or wholeness that God grants his people, which also results in harmony with God and others.

[2] **Messiah** – Transliteration of a Hebrew word meaning "anointed one," the equivalent of the Greek word *Christ*. Originally applied to anyone specially designated for a particular role, such as king or priest. Jesus himself affirmed that he was the Messiah sent from God (Matt. 16:16–17).

[3] **Ascension** – The departure of the resurrected Jesus to God the Father in heaven (Luke 24:50–51; Acts 1:1–12).

Week 7: The Case Against Israel

Micah 6:1–7:7

▲

The Lord brings charges against his people in a lawsuit, outlining their failure to remember his past deliverances and to treat one another with the kindness with which God has treated them. In particular, the wealthy have deceived and taken advantage of the weak and impoverished, but they will receive their just deserts. Because of the people's sin and the coming judgment, the city will so deteriorate that not even the closest of familial relationships will be trusted.

Guilty of forgetting their God and their neighbor, Israel will soon receive her punishment.

Reflection and Discussion

Read through the complete passage for this study, Micah 6:1–7:7. Then write your reflections on the following questions. (For further background, see the *ESV Study Bible*, pages 1704–1707; available online at www.esv.org.)

1. The Lawsuit (6:1–12)

Micah 6 opens with a kind of lawsuit in which God summons creation as his witnesses and begins to outline the indictment against his people. As evidence against them, the Lord reminds the people of his saving them from Egypt (v. 4); providing them the leadership of Moses, Aaron, and Miriam (v. 4); blessing them through the prophet Balaam, even though he had been hired by Balak to curse Israel (v. 5; compare Numbers 22–24); and bringing them into the Promised Land, crossing the Jordan River from Shittim to Gilgal (v. 5; see Joshua 2–4). What purpose in the lawsuit does mentioning these past actions have? How does this past obligate God's people in the present?

Micah 6:6–8 presents an escalating series of questions that betray Israel's attitude toward the worship of God; they view their sacrifices as the means by which they secure God's favor, as though they could buy or manipulate God with their gifts. In fact, King Ahaz, during whose reign Micah ministered (1:1), did indeed offer *his own sons* as burnt offerings (2 Chron. 28:1–4; compare Mic. 6:7). But God has already secured for the people his salvation, his constant presence, and his blessing, as shown in Micah 6:3–5! How does verse 8 contrast with the manipulations of verses 6–7? How is the response of verse 8 a more appropriate response? What does God require of his people?

Justice in the Bible includes making right decisions according to God's commands and laws, and, accordingly, to "do justice" means more than simply pursuing legal equity. Rather, doing justice includes the fair and just use of power and government to protect the weak and powerless; and, at the individual level, it includes treating one another honestly and fairly, particularly in business practices. How have the Israelites failed to do justice (vv. 9–12; see also Amos 8:4–6 and the corresponding notes in the *ESV Study Bible*)?

---

2. The Punishment (6:13–7:6)

In light of the injustice mentioned in verses 9–12, how are the punishments in 6:13–16 fitting?

In 7:1–6, the prophet piles image upon image to describe the situation in which he ministers—for example: harvest time, hunting, briers, and familial relationships. What do these images tell us about life in Israel?

---

3. Micah's Hope in the Lord (7:7)

Read Psalm 73. How is Micah able to wait for the Lord? From where does he find the confidence to know that God will hear him and save him?

Read Matthew 10:34–39, where Jesus seems to be saying that he has come to fulfill Micah 7:6. How does understanding the context of Micah 7:6 and the nature of the original message inform your understanding of what Jesus says in this passage in Matthew? In light of Micah 7, what is Jesus saying in Matthew 10:34–39?

How does Micah 7 help you understand the life and ministry of Jesus Christ?

Read through the following three sections on *Gospel Glimpses*, *Whole-Bible Connections*, and *Theological Soundings*. Then take time to consider the *Personal Implications* these sections may have for you.

Gospel Glimpses

STEADFAST LOVE. The Hebrew word variously translated as "steadfast love" (Ex. 34:6–7) or "lovingkindness"(NASB) refers to God's covenant[1] love for his people. Indeed, it is through the language of this love that God reveals himself to Moses on Mount Sinai (Ex. 34:6–7), and the psalmist notes that such love characterizes God's actions among humanity, from creation to his acts of deliverance and care (Psalm 136). It is this same love that God expects his people to show to one another ("to love kindness"; Mic. 6:8). We are to love others as God has loved us (John 13:34; 15:12).

SPIRITUAL AMNESIA. Often in the Old Testament, God speaks to his people by first reminding them that he is the God who brought them up out of Egypt (e.g., Ex. 20:2; Num. 15:41; Lev. 25:38; Judg. 6:8; Neh. 9:18; Ps. 81:10; Mic. 6:4–5), thereby reminding them of God's past deliverance. Forgetting God's past actions is intimately linked with turning away from God, especially turning away from him toward false gods (Deut. 4:9–14, 23; 6:10–15). However, the opposite is also true: remembering God's past actions strengthens our faith for today and the future.

Whole-Bible Connections

NOT PEACE, BUT A SWORD. Micah notes that the end of Israel will include a time of suffering such that even close familial relationships will be divided. This becomes a picture of the end of time: before the future age of peace, there will be a time of suffering. With the coming of Jesus Christ to earth, his use of this text to describe his ministry points to his bringing about this foretold end of time, characterized by division between those who follow him and those who reject him, even within the same family. Jesus' bringing of the sword also reminds the church that this is not yet the age of peace. That final age will come after this life of suffering, when King Jesus returns.

WAITING FOR THE LORD. Even before the Assyrians and Babylonians brought destruction, exile, and suffering to the people of God, their Lord promised their future rescue (Mic. 7:7). This promise of future rescue will sustain them through exile and give them the courage they need to endure (Jer. 29:1–14; Dan. 9:1–2). Similarly, the New Testament promises a future deliverance for God's people, and this promise gives us courage to endure suffering in the present (2 Cor. 4:7–18). In the meantime, we wait for the Lord, making use of his Word, prayer, and the sacraments to strengthen and encourage us.

Theological Soundings

GRACE AND WORKS. Unlike with the pagans surrounding the nation of Israel, who believed that they needed to somehow attract their gods' attention, earn their favor, or manipulate them into action, the God of Israel initiated contact with his people. He called Abram out of Haran (Gen. 12:1–4) and pursued his people in Egypt to bring them out and take them to the land of Canaan. It was only after he pursued and rescued his people that he brought them to Mount Sinai and gave them the law.[2] Their worship and obedience to the law was a response to God's initiating, saving grace, not a means of earning it.

OBLIGATION. Though our lives of obedience are a response to God's pursuing, initiating grace, we are, nevertheless, obligated to such responses. Images of such obligation throughout the Bible include that of a wife being faithful to her husband (Jeremiah 2–3; Hosea 2) and of slaves or servants obeying their masters (Rom. 6:15–23). Indeed, because of the grace of God, we are indebted to the Spirit (Rom. 8:12–17) and have been bought with the blood of Jesus (1 Cor. 6:20)—realities that obligate us to live according to the Spirit and to glorify God with our bodies, respectively. Conclusively, Jesus says, "If you love me, you will keep my commandments" (John 14:15).

Personal Implications

Take time to reflect on the implications of Micah 6:1–7:7 for your own life today. Consider what you have learned that might lead you to praise God, repent of sin, and trust in his gracious promises. Write down your reflections under the three headings we have considered and on the passage as a whole.

1. Gospel Glimpses

2. Whole-Bible Connections

3. Theological Soundings

4. Micah 6:1–7:7

> ### As You Finish This Unit . . .

Take a moment now to ask for the Lord's blessing and help as you continue in this study of Jonah, Micah, and Nahum. And take a moment also to look back through this unit of study, to reflect on some key things that the Lord may be teaching you.

Definitions

[1] **Covenant** – A binding agreement between two parties, typically involving a formal statement of their relationship, a list of stipulations and obligations for both parties, a list of witnesses to the agreement, and a list of curses for unfaithfulness and blessings for faithfulness to the agreement. The OT is more properly understood as the old covenant, meaning the agreement established between God and his people prior to the coming of Jesus Christ and the establishment of the new covenant (NT).

[2] **Law** – When spelled with an initial capital letter, "Law" refers to the first five books of the Bible. The Law contains numerous commands of God to his people, including the Ten Commandments and instructions regarding worship, sacrifice, and life in Israel. The NT often uses "the law" (lower case) to refer to the entire body of precepts set forth in the books of the Law.

WEEK 8: GOD'S STEADFAST LOVE

Micah 7:8–20

▲

The Place of the Passage

Israel as she awaits her judgment is like a prisoner of war in a dark dungeon awaiting the completion of his sentence. The image turns from a prison to the entire ancient world, as God brings Israel out of the dungeon and back to the Promised Land, which he will enlarge from sea to sea and mountain to mountain. All of God's people will dwell secure in the city of God, and those who remain outside will be destroyed by the judgment of God. After imaging Israel's restoration in terms of a new exodus, akin to the first exodus[1] out of Egypt, the book of Micah ends with a beautiful passage describing God's forgiveness of his people's sin.

The Big Picture

The Lord forgives and rescues his people from their sin and from sin's consequences.

Reflection and Discussion

Read through the complete passage for this study, Micah 7:8–20. Then write your reflections on the following questions. (For further background, see the *ESV Study Bible*, pages 1707–1708; available online at www.esv.org.)

1. The Discipline of Israel (7:8–10)

The discipline of Israel through defeat at the hands of Assyria and Babylon is depicted as Israel's being like a war prisoner in a dark dungeon. The prisoner acknowledges the justice of the discipline: it is "because I have sinned" (v. 9). Nevertheless, even though the discipline is just and is a result of sin, the Lord remains present as the hope of the city. Note in the space below the various actions of the Lord toward his people in the midst of the dungeon (vv. 8–10). How should this help us to see God's favor toward his people even in the midst of their sin?

In the ancient world, it was believed that military battles between nations reflected the cosmic battle between those nations' gods. The victorious army, therefore, believed that their god was the stronger god, as evidenced by their army's victory (compare 1 Sam. 5:1–5). How does this help us to understand the taunting of the nations who conquer Israel (Mic. 7:10; compare 4:11)?

Israel sinned against God; therefore, God brought the Assyrians and Babylonians to execute his judgment against Israel. At first glance, then, it may seem unfair that God would turn and judge those nations for doing his bidding. How does this taunting help us to make sense of God's judgment of Assyria and Babylon (see Jer. 50:11 and the corresponding notes in the *ESV Study Bible*)?

2. The Restoration of Israel (7:11–20)

How do verses 11–13 anticipate a fulfillment of Israel's mission (see "The Mission of Israel" under "Whole-Bible Connections" in Week 6)? How do these verses anticipate judgment on those who do not turn to the Lord?

Review the Shepherd-King passages of Micah: 2:12–13; 4:1–5; 5:2–6; 7:14–17. Summarize what you learn about the Shepherd-King from this book.

Why is Israel's future deliverance from Assyria and Babylon pictured in terms of their original deliverance from Egypt (v. 15)?

Record below all of the words, phrases, and images used in verses 18–20 to describe how God treats the sins of his people.

What reasons do those verses give for God's forgiveness of his people's sin?

Spend some time meditating on verses 18–20, on what God does with our sin, and on why he treats it in this way. Then spend time giving thanks to God and worshiping him for his forgiveness. Use the space below, if you wish, to write a prayer, song, or poem of thanksgiving.

Read through the following three sections on *Gospel Glimpses, Whole-Bible Connections,* and *Theological Soundings*. Then take time to consider the *Personal Implications* these sections may have for you.

Gospel Glimpses

CONFESSION. When our hearts respond to the Word of God, that response will be accompanied by an outward or public confession. Confession, as in Micah 7:9, is an acknowledgment of sin: we are to confess our sins to God (Ezra 10:1; 1 John 1:9) and to each other (James 5:16). Confession is also a product and evidence of faith by which we confirm our heart's response to the gospel, even to ourselves (Rom. 10:8–13).

DISCIPLINE. Sin has consequences (Mic. 7:9). Sometimes those consequences are simply the natural effects of our sin and the hurt and pain that sin causes us and others; sometimes those consequences are the discipline of God. However, even such suffering because of our sin is an act of love from God, because, like a good father, he disciplines his children (Deut. 8:5), and such discipline proves his love for us (Prov. 3:11–12). Moreover, such discipline from God is for our good, that we might share in God's own holiness[2] (Heb. 12:3–11).

FORGIVENESS. Having confessed their sin (Mic. 7:9), the Lord's people are promised forgiveness, a forgiveness that pardons, passes over, treads upon, and casts away our sin. Such complete and total forgiveness is possible only through the life, death, and resurrection of Jesus Christ, who paid the penalty of death that we deserve (Rom. 6:23), shed his blood for our forgiveness (Heb. 9:14), and cleanses us from all unrighteousness[3] (1 John 1:7, 9).

Whole-Bible Connections

NEW EXODUS. The deliverance of God's people out of Babylon is described in terms of a new exodus, akin to the first exodus out of Egypt (Mic. 7:15;

compare Isa. 11:11–12; Jer. 16:14–15). This new exodus was foretold in terms of a total renewal of Israel, complete with a return to the land and even a new covenant and a new law (Jer. 31:31–40). This new exodus/new covenant/new law image finds ultimate fulfillment in the life and ministry of Jesus Christ (Heb. 12:18–25). Jesus, our Passover[4] Lamb who secured our salvation from the slavery of sin and death (John 8:34–38; Rev. 5:9–10), comes as one greater than Moses (Heb. 3:1–6), fulfills the law (Matt. 5:17–48), and institutes the new covenant through his blood (Mark 14:24; Heb. 9:11–28).

▶ Theological Soundings

FINAL VINDICATION. Micah 7:9 anticipates Israel's return from exile as a public vindication in which the enemies of God's people see the Lord powerfully rescue his people, demonstrating both his strength and his ownership of his people. That vindication after exile anticipates the final vindication of God's people at the end of time, when Christ will return to claim his people as his bride and execute judgment against his and our enemies.

GOD'S INHERITANCE. The Bible speaks not only of the inheritance God promises for his people but also of his own inheritance (Mic. 7:14). This inheritance is his people themselves; that is, his relationship with us is what God anticipates and enjoys throughout eternity. God's people are his "portion" or "inheritance" among the nations in the Old Testament (e.g., Deut. 32:9; Zech. 2:12), with echoes of the same in the New Testament, where those who have been given new life in Jesus Christ are called God's "glorious inheritance" (Eph. 1:18).

▶ Personal Implications

Take time to reflect on the implications of Micah 7:8–20 for your own life today. Consider what you have learned that might lead you to praise God, repent of sin, and trust in his gracious promises. Write down your reflections under the three headings we have considered and on the passage as a whole.

1. Gospel Glimpses

2. Whole-Bible Connections

3. Theological Soundings

4. Micah 7:8–20

> ## As You Finish This Unit . . .

Take a moment now to ask for the Lord's blessing and help as you continue in this study of Jonah, Micah, and Nahum. And take a moment also to look back through this unit of study, to reflect on some key things that the Lord may be teaching you.

Definitions

[1] **Exodus** – The departure of the people of Israel from Egypt and their journey to Mount Sinai under Moses' leadership (Exodus 1–19; Numbers 33). The exodus demonstrated God's power and providence for his people, who had been enslaved by the Egyptians. The annual festival of Passover commemorates God's final plague upon the Egyptians, resulting in the Israelites' release from Egypt.

[2] **Holiness** – A quality possessed by something or someone set apart for special use. When applied to God, it refers to his utter perfection and complete transcendence over creation. God's people are called to imitate his holiness (Lev. 19:2), which means being set apart from sin and reserved for his purposes.

[3] **Righteousness** – The quality of being morally right and without sin. One of God's distinctive attributes. God imputes righteousness to (justifies) those who trust in Jesus Christ. "Unrighteousness" describes the absence of righteousness, or behavior contrary to or absent of righteousness.

[4] **Passover** – An annual Israelite festival commemorating God's final plague on the Egyptians, which led to the exodus. In this final plague, the Lord "passed over" the houses of those who spread the blood of a lamb on the doorposts of their homes (Exodus 12). Those who did not obey this command suffered the death of their firstborn.

WEEK 9: THE DIVINE WARRIOR

Nahum 1:1–15

▲

The Place of the Passage

The book of Nahum opens with a psalm of praise in honor of God, who, like a warrior, comes to avenge the wrongs committed against his people. This warrior God will decimate the Assyrian Empire, which, though at the peak of its power, with innumerable armies at its disposal, will be destroyed as quickly as dry vegetation burns. This judgment[1] comes from the goodness of the Lord, who saves those who hide and wait in him. For them, the coming of this warrior God is indeed good news of peace.

The Big Picture

The Lord, our mighty warrior, comes to rescue his people by defeating the Assyrians and decimating their capital city, Nineveh.

> ## Reflection and Discussion

Read through the complete passage for this study, Nahum 1:1–15. Then write your reflections on the following questions. (For further background, see the *ESV Study Bible*, pages 1712–1714; available online at www.esv.org.)

1. The Lord Is a Warrior (1:1–8)

Nahum opens with a psalm of praise to the Lord. What do we learn about God in verses 2–8?

The Assyrians completed their destruction of the northern kingdom of Israel in 722 BC. This means they have been oppressing the southern kingdom for more than 60 years (see the "Introduction to Nahum" in the *ESV Study Bible*, page 1709). As God's people cry out to him for deliverance, it may feel like God is slow to act. How do these verses address that slowness?

Read 2 Peter 3:1–13. How does that passage and Nahum 1:2–8 inform our understanding of God's apparent slowness in keeping his promises of judgment against the wicked?

Amid these verses describing the power, vengeance, and wrath of God, Nahum jarringly turns to exclaim, "The LORD is good" (v. 7). Why do you think the goodness of the Lord is mentioned here?

What does it mean that God is a "stronghold" and "refuge"? What does it mean that he "knows" those who take refuge in him (v. 7)? See also Psalm 27 and the corresponding notes in the *ESV Study Bible*.

2. The Defeat of Nineveh (1:9–15)

The Assyrian Empire was likely at the height of its power, with a massive army and seemingly endless resources for conquest, during the ministry of Nahum (see v. 12 and the corresponding notes in the *ESV Study Bible*). How do the images of Nineveh's destruction in verse 10 emphasize the power and might of Israel's God?

Why does the Lord mention the cutting off of images from Nineveh in verse 14? What does such action represent?

What message is being communicated to God's own people through this cutting off of Nineveh's gods and images?

The note on verse 15 in the *ESV Study Bible* explains the image in this verse as the running of a messenger from a battle, coming home to proclaim the good news of the destruction of Nineveh (see 2 Sam. 18:24–27 for an example of this announcement of victory). How does this picture inform our understanding of the apostle Paul's use of this imagery in Romans 10:14–17?

Read through the following three sections on *Gospel Glimpses, Whole-Bible Connections*, and *Theological Soundings*. Then take time to consider the *Personal Implications* these sections may have for you.

Gospel Glimpses

GOD KNOWS HIS PEOPLE. God's knowing of his people consists of more than his knowledge of information about them; it includes the intimacy of their belonging to him (Nah. 1:7). In Numbers 16, God distinguishes between the rebels of Korah and God's high priest Aaron with the statement, "In the morning the LORD will show who is his" (Num. 16:5; see ESV footnote), that is, who belongs to him. Jesus takes up this same language, noting that he knows those who belong to him, and they know him; his sheep hear his voice; he knows them, and they follow him (John 10:7–30). Those who belong to God are those whom God has known from the beginning (Eph. 1:4), those for whom Jesus died (John 10:15; 1 Cor. 7:23), and those who respond to the good news of Jesus Christ with faith (John 1:12).

Whole-Bible Connections

WARRIOR GOD. The Bible often makes use of cultural language and images to convey God's message of salvation for his people (see Nah. 1:2–5). The ancient world's cultural images of gods battling the monsters of chaos are sometimes deployed in the Bible to show God's might and power over the cosmos. For example, Psalm 18 uses this language to depict God as a warrior coming in fury to rescue his servant David. This warrior-God language variously depicts God's salvation of his people, his fighting against his own people in judgment, and his kingly rule over his people.

YOKE. A yoke is a wooden crosspiece placed on the necks of two animals and then attached to a cart or plow so that together the animals may pull it. As an everyday tool for a farming community like Israel, the yoke naturally became a picture of the burden placed upon the people by a parent, ruler, or teacher. For example, the people complained that Solomon's rule had become too heavy of a yoke for them (1 Kings 12:4), and the rule of Assyria became a heavy yoke for the people also (see Nah. 1:13 and the corresponding note in the *ESV Study Bible*). The yoke was used to describe voluntary slavery (1 Tim. 6:1) and even interpersonal relationships (2 Cor. 6:14–7:1). The prophet Jeremiah made and wore a yoke to prophesy the coming exile at the hands of Babylon.

Theological Soundings

THE SLOWNESS OF GOD. Amid suffering, it can sometimes feel as though God is slow to act, slow to rescue, slow to heal, or slow to judge the wicked. In fact, this apparent slowness leads the psalmist to cry out, "How long, O LORD?" and to express feelings of being forgotten or abandoned by God (Ps. 13:1). However, the Bible explains that God is "merciful and gracious, slow to anger, and abounding in steadfast love and faithfulness" (Ex. 34:6; compare Nah. 1:3). His slowness allows opportunity for the wicked to turn back to him for mercy[2] and for people in their suffering to trust in God's promises. Even so, he "will by no means clear the guilty" (Ex. 34:7), guaranteeing a day of reckoning for those who persist in their rebellion and a day of salvation for those who continue to wait for him.

THE SUPREMACY OF GOD. As noted in the "Reflection and Discussion" section of Week 8, in the ancient world it was believed that the gods of nations at war fought and determined the outcome of the human military battles. The victorious army represented and proclaimed the victorious god. This ancient cultural understanding is taken up by the Bible to proclaim the God of Israel's supremacy over all other gods. In Nahum 1:14, the prophet proclaims the Lord's power over the Assyrian gods not only by defeating them but also by casting them out of their own temple. In Jeremiah, the prophet demonstrates the Lord's power over the Babylonian gods by capturing them and putting them to shame (Jer. 50:1–2). In the New Testament, this language continues through the conquering of the powers of evil (Col. 2:15) and through the destruction of the dragon in Revelation 12.

Personal Implications

Take time to reflect on the implications of Nahum 1:1–15 for your own life today. Consider what you have learned that might lead you to praise God, repent of sin, and trust in his gracious promises. Write down your reflections under the three headings we have considered and on the passage as a whole.

1. Gospel Glimpses

2. Whole-Bible Connections

3. Theological Soundings

4. Nahum 1:1–15

As You Finish This Unit . . .

Take a moment now to ask for the Lord's blessing and help as you continue in this study of Jonah, Micah, and Nahum. And take a moment also to look back through this unit of study, to reflect on some key things that the Lord may be teaching you.

Definitions

[1] **Judgment** – An assessment of something or someone, especially moral assessment. The Bible also speaks of a final day of judgment when Christ returns, when all those who have refused to repent will be judged (Rev. 20:12–15).

[2] **Mercy** – Compassion and kindness toward someone experiencing hardship, sometimes even when such suffering results from the person's own sin or foolishness. God displays mercy toward his people and they, in turn, are called to display mercy toward others (Luke 6:36).

WEEK 10: BEHOLD, I AM AGAINST YOU

Nahum 2:1–13

▲

The Place of the Passage

Nahum continues his proclamation against the Assyrians, and their capital city of Nineveh in particular, with a detailed description of the fall of the city. With vivid and sensory detail, the prophet invites the reader to witness the invasion of Nineveh, which begins with an assault on the city walls, moves into the city proper, includes a looting of the city treasuries, and concludes with the destruction of the palace itself. This devastation occurs because the Lord himself is against the Assyrians and is restoring the majesty of Israel.

The Big Picture

The den of Assyrian lions, Nineveh, is plundered by the Lord as he restores the majesty of Israel.

► **Reflection and Discussion**

Read through the complete passage for this study, Nahum 2:1–13. Then write your reflections on the following questions. (For further background, see the *ESV Study Bible*, pages 1715–1716; available online at www.esv.org.)

1. The Great Reversal of Nineveh (2:1, 3–13)

Just as the Assyrians plundered the nations they conquered, especially Israel, the army coming against Nineveh will plunder that city. How do verses 4–5 revel in that plundering of Israel's enemies?

The language of Nahum 2 invites the reader to experience the destruction of Nineveh fully. Record some of the ways the chapter engages the reader's senses.

Why does the prophet invite the reader into such a full experience of this vision? How would such a text inspire the faith of God's people, who are awaiting the restoration of the majesty of Israel?

The Assyrian kings were known for their self-praise over their various conquests; they bragged about the violence and terror they inflicted upon their enemies, and they boasted of the lavish wealth they accumulated from their conquests and the tributes they demanded from their vassals.[1] How do these verses fittingly show the reversal of Assyria's prosperity?

Read 2 Kings 18:13–35. Summarize the boasting of the Rabshakeh.

How does the Rabshakeh's message to the people within Jerusalem help our understanding of Nahum 2:13?

2. The Great Restoration of Israel (2:2)

The promise of God to Abraham to make him into a great nation and give him the land of Canaan was, in many ways, finally complete during the glory days of King David and his son Solomon. In those days, God's people had possession of the land, were unified as a nation, and finally experienced peace and stability. The majesty of Israel, however, lasted only a generation, as Solomon's successors tore the kingdom into two; over the subsequent generations, the two kingdoms continued to devolve and to suffer God's judgment until only the southern kingdom of Judah was left. In light of this history, what does it mean that "the LORD is restoring the majesty of Jacob as the majesty of Israel"?

Read Genesis 32:22–32; 35:9–15, and the corresponding notes in the *ESV Study Bible*, especially the note on 32:28. How does the spiritual change (and resulting name change) in Jacob help us further to understand Nahum 2:2?

Read through the following three sections on *Gospel Glimpses*, *Whole-Bible Connections*, and *Theological Soundings*. Then take time to consider the *Personal Implications* these sections may have for you.

Gospel Glimpses

LION LEADERS. The Assyrian kings often decorated their palaces and cities with images of lions; they also described themselves as lions and even behaved like lions in the violence they enacted upon their captives (Nah. 2:11–12). Such lion imagery was common in the ancient world as a symbol of royalty or rule, and later Jeremiah would describe Babylon's king using this same image (Jer. 50:17; 51:38). Moreover, this image of a ruling, conquering lion was used to describe a descendant of Judah (Gen. 49:8–12), anticipating both the conquest and rule of King David and eventually the Messiah. Accordingly, this image—the lion of the tribe of Judah—is applied to the Lord Jesus Christ, who conquers and rules as that long-awaited descendant of King David (Rev. 5:5).

Whole-Bible Connections

TAUNTING. As in Nahum 2, the prophets often use taunting or a mock lament to proclaim the destruction of the Lord's enemies. For example, Isaiah 16:6–7 heralds the fall of Moab through a call for everyone to wail and mourn, especially for the loss of raisin cakes from one of Moab's major cities; and Jeremiah 51:8–9 employs a mock lament by calling Babylon's allies to come and try to heal her. This same taunting is also employed in the New Testament when, for example, Paul employs Old Testament texts to proclaim victory over death through the resurrection of Jesus Christ (1 Cor. 15:54b–55).

NAME CHANGE. Occasionally in the Bible, God changes the name of a person. For example, Abram becomes Abraham (Gen. 17:5), and Sarai becomes Sarah (Gen. 17:15). These name changes typically denote a change in the individual's spiritual maturity or relationship to God, signaling a new calling or mission from the Lord. Other examples include Jacob becoming Israel (Gen. 32:28; 35:10; compare Nah. 2:2) and Simon becoming Peter (John 1:42). This name change finds expression at the end of time, when God's people are given a white stone with a new name on it, perhaps corresponding to the new identity we have in Jesus Christ (Rev. 2:17; compare 2 Cor. 5:17).

TREASURE. The gold, silver, and other precious items from the temple of the Lord are used occasionally in the Bible as representative of God himself through their association with the temple. Perhaps partly due to the pagan notion that the spirit of a god was present in images or representations of that god, the removal of these various vessels by the nations who conquered Israel represented to those conquerors the defeat of Israel's God by the gods of those conquering nations. For example, in 2 Kings 18:16, 22, Hezekiah's stripping of the gold from the temple is used by the Rabshakeh as evidence of the Lord's powerlessness; and, in Daniel 1:2, the items from the Lord's temple are taken as representative tribute to Babylon's gods. Accordingly, the plundering of Nineveh in Nahum 2:9, in light of 1:14, likely alludes to the Lord's defeat of Assyria's gods.

Theological Soundings

DEPRAVITY. Sin's corruption of humanity is often spoken of in terms of "total" depravity[2] rather than "complete" or "absolute" depravity. Total depravity refers to the effect of sin's corruption upon every aspect of every human: thoughts, feelings, desires, and actions. However, though sin distorts and ruins every part of us, we are not as bad as we could be; in other words, we are not completely or absolutely depraved. Even so, every once in a while God gives us a glimpse of what such complete or absolute depravity might look like through the actions of such examples as Assyria, Nazi Germany, and more recent regimes of complete wickedness.

THE TERROR OF THE LORD. Popular theology often misconstrues the battle between God and Satan[3] as a battle between two equal or nearly equal forces, each vying for absolute rule. This perspective on the cosmic forces does not, however, reflect the reality given to us in Scripture. The Bible makes clear that there is only one absolute power, the Lord God Almighty. Satan is subject to him (Job 1:12), and Satan's darkness cannot overcome him (John 1:5). Indeed, what could be more terrifying than to hear not once but twice from Almighty God, "I am against you" (Nah. 2:13; 3:5)? Indeed, "It is a fearful thing to fall into the hands of the living God" (Heb. 10:31).

Personal Implications

Take time to reflect on the implications of Nahum 2:1–13 for your own life today. Consider what you have learned that might lead you to praise God, repent of sin, and trust in his gracious promises. Write down your reflections under the three headings we have considered and on the passage as a whole.

1. Gospel Glimpses

2. Whole-Bible Connections

3. Theological Soundings

4. Nahum 2:1–13

> ### As You Finish This Unit . . .

Take a moment now to ask for the Lord's blessing and help as you continue in this study of Jonah, Micah, and Nahum. And take a moment also to look back through this unit of study, to reflect on some key things that the Lord may be teaching you.

Definitions

[1] **Vassal** – A subservient power who has accepted the terms of a covenant treaty with a superior power. Such treaties usually required the vassal to pledge loyalty to the superior power and to present a monetary tribute.

[2] **Depravity** – The sinful condition of human nature apart from grace, whereby humans are inclined to serve their own will and desires and to reject God's rule.

[3] **Satan** – A spiritual being whose name means "accuser." As the leader of all the demonic forces, he opposes God's rule and seeks to harm God's people and accuse them of wrongdoing. His power, however, is confined to the bounds that God has set for him, and one day he will be destroyed along with all his demons (Matt. 25:41; Rev. 20:10).

Week 11: The Shame of Sin

Nahum 3:1–19

This last chapter of the book of Nahum graphically depicts the destruction and resulting shame of the Assyrian Empire. Beginning with an explanation of Nineveh's guilt, the prophet once again invites the reader into the vision to witness the soldiers slaying the Ninevites; then the scene turns to portray the city as a prostitute whose nakedness is exposed and covered in filth. As a further attack against Nineveh's haughty self-confidence, the city is compared to the city of Thebes; once considered indestructible, that Egyptian city was conquered by the Assyrians themselves. In like manner, Nineveh, who trusts so much in her own fortifications and innumerable army, will also fall because of her unceasing evil.

The Big Picture

Nineveh's unceasing evil leads to her destruction and resulting shame, reminding us of the future exposure of our deeds and even our motives, and calling us to cling to the Lord while he yet remains patient.

> ### Reflection and Discussion

Read through the complete passage for this study, Nahum 3:1–19. Then write your reflections on the following questions. (For further background, see the *ESV Study Bible*, pages 1716–1718; available online at www.esv.org.)

1. The Sin of Nineveh (3:1, 4, 19)

Review 2:2, 12; 3:1, 4, and 19. What is the sin of Nineveh? Why is she being destroyed?

Read Hebrews 10:26–31. In the book of Jonah, we saw that Nineveh had received a warning of judgment from the Lord, and, in response, the king and people of the city repented and received mercy and forgiveness (Jonah 3:10). How does Hebrews 10:26–31, the history of Nineveh's repentance, and Nineveh's present wickedness add to our understanding of God's judgment here?

---

2. The Shame of Nineveh (3:2–3, 5–7)

Three different words are used in verse 3 for the slain in Nineveh: "corpses" refers to people fatally wounded; "dead bodies" refers to those who have collapsed from exhaustion; and "bodies" comes from the word that refers to the back of the body, likely representing their lying facedown on the ground. Why does the prophet emphasize the violence done to Nineveh? How would this impact the Israelite reader's trust in the word of God through Nahum?

Read Isaiah 66:18–24. How do those verses help make sense of the graphic language used in Nahum 3:5–7?

How are these explicit verses a fitting picture of the judgment of Nineveh? How does this external shame fit the exposure of her heart and deeds before the holiness of God?

3. The Former Strength of Nineveh (3:8–16)

Review the notes on the apparent invincibility of Thebes (vv. 8–9) in the *ESV Study Bible*, page 1717. The Assyrians themselves witnessed the fortifications of Thebes as they marched against that city and conquered it, despite its rumored invincibility. How does the defeat of Thebes add certainty to the prophecy against Nineveh? How would the reference to Thebes bolster the faith of the Israelite reader?

Review verses 12–16 and the corresponding notes in the *ESV Study Bible*, pages 1717–1718. What is the strength of Nineveh? In what is Nineveh trusting?

In the war-torn world of Nahum's time, Israel was desperately attempting to find her own source of strength and safety, variously making alliances with neighboring nations and willingly seeking peace with Assyria through tribute, only to attempt later a rebellion against the occupying government. How do these verses call Israel away from trusting in the same things that the powerful nations around them relied upon (see Ps. 20:7–8)?

4. A Summary of Nineveh (3:17–19)

The last word of Nahum in the original Hebrew is the word "unceasing." How is this a fitting word with which to conclude the book, as it refers both to the

Assyrians' evil and also to God's patience or slowness to bring judgment against them (Nah. 1:3; compare Ex. 34:6)?

....

....

....

....

....

....

Read through the following three sections on *Gospel Glimpses*, *Whole-Bible Connections*, and *Theological Soundings*. Then take time to consider the *Personal Implications* these sections may have for you.

Gospel Glimpses

EXPOSING OUR SHAME. Nineveh's judgment climaxes with a picture of her most private parts being exposed as she stands before the world covered in filth. This graphic image points to the end of time, when all people will have all of their secrets exposed—not only their deeds done in darkness but even the hidden "purposes of the heart" (1 Cor. 4:5). For those who trust in the life, death, and resurrection of Jesus Christ, however, Jesus himself provides the covering for our exposure: his own righteousness (Zech. 3:1–5; Matt. 22:1–14; Rev. 7:13–17).

THE ISOLATION OF HELL. As a result of her judgment, Nineveh finds herself utterly alone, with no one even to grieve for her (Nah. 3:7). Such isolation portrays the destitution of eternity for those who reject God and his Son, our Savior. As the Egyptians found themselves in total darkness because of Pharaoh's refusal to heed the word of the Lord from Moses (Ex. 10:21–23), so too will those who reject Christ be cast into utter darkness (Matt. 8:12; 25:30). It is this very isolation that Jesus endures on the cross for his people, as he cries out, "My God, my God, why have you forsaken me?" (Matt. 27:46).

THE SHAME OF THE CROSS. Our sin not only results in our guilt before God; it also brings with it the feelings of shame associated with that guilt. As we see with the destruction of Nineveh, her punishment includes becoming the object of scorn of those who see her and mock her (Nah. 2:10–12) or shrink away from her in disgust and horror (3:7). That shame provides us an image of the spiritual shame we experience in being alienated from God through our disobedience. But the good news of the gospel is that Jesus Christ carried our shame on the cross. To be crucified naked, especially for a circumcised[1] Jew in a Gentile culture, would result in scorn, mockery, and alienation. But, for our sake, Jesus "endured the cross, despising the shame" (Heb. 12:2); therefore, those in Christ "shall never again be put to shame" (Joel 2:26–27).

Whole-Bible Connections

PROSTITUTION. Although the image of adultery or prostitution is most often used to describe Israel's turning away from the Lord to false gods (e.g., Ezekiel 16 and 23), it is also used as an image of those who, like the adulteress in Proverbs 7, lead God's people astray, wooing them with grace and charms but in reality luring them into destruction and death (Nah. 3:4). This picture is taken up by the book of Revelation to depict those who are enticed by the world's promises of wealth and pleasure (Revelation 17–18).

ORACLES OF WOE. The prophets often use oracles of woe to announce judgment (see Nah. 3:1); in fact, every prophetic book of the Bible except for Hosea uses the woe oracle, and these oracles follow a similar pattern, beginning the announcement with "woe," followed by the recipient of the judgment; for example, "Woe to you who. . . ." Then the woe oracle typically contains either an explanation of the evidence against the recipient of the woe or a description of the coming judgment, or sometimes both. Jesus also utilizes the woe oracle, particularly against the scribes[2] and Pharisees[3] (see Matt. 23:1–36 and Luke 11:37–52).

Theological Soundings

HISTORY AND THE BIBLE. Historical references in the Bible, such as those in Nahum 3:8–10, remind us of the authenticity and reliability of God's Word. It is not a text outside of time and space but one written within the confines of history, revealing a God who interacts with the world and the people in it. Furthermore, details such as city names and sites, rulers, wars, and even cultural references such as navigational details provide us with verifiable specifics that reinforce our faith in the truthfulness of God's Word.

CONTINUALLY PATIENT. The last word of Nahum reminds us of the beginning of the book, which references God's long-suffering patience. Such patience, which led to the Ninevites' previous repentance and mercy from the Lord, reminds us of God's present patience, as he calls all people to turn to him away from their sin so that they too might find his mercy and forgiveness. Those who ignore God's patience and instead remain continually in their sin, as the Ninevites did, will find that God's patience will indeed one day run out.

> ## Personal Implications

Take time to reflect on the implications of Nahum 3:1–19 for your own life today. Consider what you have learned that might lead you to praise God, repent of sin, and trust in his gracious promises. Write down your reflections under the three headings we have considered and on the passage as a whole.

1. Gospel Glimpses

2. Whole-Bible Connections

3. Theological Soundings

4. Nahum 3:1–19

As You Finish This Unit . . .

Take a moment now to ask for the Lord's blessing and help as you continue in this study of Jonah, Micah, and Nahum. And take a moment also to look back through this unit of study, to reflect on some key things that the Lord may be teaching you.

Definitions

[1] **Circumcision** – The ritual practice of removing the foreskin of an individual, which was commanded for all male Israelites in OT times as a sign of participation in the covenant that God had established with Abraham.

[2] **Scribe** – Someone trained and authorized to transcribe, teach, and interpret the Scriptures. Jesus often criticized scribes for their pride, their legalistic approach to the Scriptures, and their refusal to believe in him.

[3] **Pharisee** – A member of a popular religious/political party in NT times characterized by strict adherence to the law of Moses and also to extrabiblical Jewish traditions. The Pharisees were frequently criticized by Jesus for their legalistic and hypocritical practices. The apostle Paul was a zealous Pharisee prior to his conversion.

WEEK 12: SUMMARY AND CONCLUSION

▲

We conclude our study of Jonah, Micah, and Nahum by summarizing the big picture of God's message through these books. Then we will consider several questions in order to reflect on various Gospel Glimpses, Whole-Bible Connections, and Theological Soundings throughout the entire study.

The Big Picture of Jonah, Micah, and Nahum

As Moses stood on Mount Sinai in the presence of God, the Lord descended in a cloud and appeared before him, proclaiming his name to Moses: "The LORD, the LORD, a God merciful and gracious, slow to anger, and abounding in steadfast love and faithfulness, keeping steadfast love for thousands, forgiving iniquity and transgression and sin, but who will by no means clear the guilty" (Ex. 34:6–7). Jonah, Micah, and Nahum demonstrate this character of God through his explanation of world events occurring during their ministries.

In the ministry of Jonah, God's slowness to anger and abundance of love and forgiveness is shown both in his forgiveness of the Ninevites when they repent of their sin and turn to the Lord and also in his pursuit of Jonah. After running from obedience to the Lord, Jonah struggles—like the rest of Israel—with the very compassion of God: how could God forgive the sins of his people's enemies?

God's pursuit of his people and the manifestation of his character continues through the prophecies of Micah. In his ministry we see some of the limits of God's patience, as he does not "clear the guilty," even among his own people. Because of the abuses of power among the leaders of God's people, the Lord will bring the Assyrians and the Babylonians to discipline Israel for her guilt. Even so, God remains eager to forgive iniquity and transgression and sin, promising a day of deliverance in which the Savior, like a shepherd and king, will gather the flock of God, rule over it, and bring it peace.

But woe to the enemies of God and his people! Nahum proclaims that the Lord who does not "clear the guilty" will bring devastation upon the Assyrian Empire, represented by its capital city of Nineveh. Assyria trampled underfoot the forgiveness of God they had known in the days of Jonah, and they plundered God's very people. Add to these crimes their violence, deceit, and general wickedness, and their judgment is as sure as their own past victory over Thebes.

Gospel Glimpses

In addition to reminding us that God rules over and directs the nations for his own purposes, these three books remind us of the very character of God, who is slow to anger and eager to forgive, but who will not clear the guilty. Accordingly, Jonah, Micah, and Nahum call us to wait for the Lord our refuge in times of distress, to turn back to him wherever we have turned away, to trust in the salvation of our Shepherd-King, and to expect the coming judgment of God, when those who hide in him will be saved while those who reject his forgiveness and salvation will be cast out into the desolation and isolation of darkness.

How have Jonah, Micah, and Nahum brought new clarity to your understanding of the gospel?

What particular passages or themes in Jonah, Micah, and Nahum have led you to a fresh understanding and grasp of God's grace to us through Jesus?

Whole-Bible Connections

These three books highlight the mission of God's people to proclaim the good news of God's salvation to all nations on earth. This was Israel's original call—to be a blessing to all nations—and it remains the church's call to go and make disciples of all nations. The urgency of this call is the limit of God's patience, for a day is coming when the King will return to gather his people from all over the world and execute judgment against all of his and our enemies.

How has this study of Jonah, Micah, and Nahum filled out your understanding of the biblical storyline of redemption?

What themes emphasized in Jonah, Micah, and Nahum have helped you deepen your grasp of the Bible's unity?

What passages or themes have expanded your understanding of the redemption that Jesus provides, begun at his first coming and consummated at his return?

What connections between these books and the New Testament were new to you?

Theological Soundings

Through our study together, we have learned much about God: his rule and power over creation, his supremacy over the so-called gods of other nations, his relentless pursuit of his people, and his mission to spread his good news of salvation to all nations. We have also learned of the nature and trustworthiness of his Word: despite the false prophets who seek to suppress it, God's Word confirms itself internally and is verified by the events of world history, which confirm it externally. Additionally, we have learned more about God's salvation of mankind: the union of grace and good works; the obligation of God's people to obey their Lord; and the nature of pure, undefiled religion.

How has your theology been refined during the course of studying Jonah, Micah, and Nahum?

How has your understanding of the nature and character of God been deepened throughout this study?

What unique contributions do Jonah, Micah, and Nahum make toward our understanding of who Jesus is and what he has accomplished through his life, death, and resurrection?

What specifically do Jonah, Micah, and Nahum teach us about the human condition and our need of redemption?

Personal Implications

God gave us the books of Jonah, Micah, and Nahum, ultimately, to transform us into the likeness of his Son. If our study of this letter does not strengthen our communion with God and worship of him, we have been wasting our time. As you reflect on our study of Jonah, Micah, and Nahum as a whole, what implications do you see for your life?

What life implications flow from your reflections on the questions already asked in this week's study concerning Gospel Glimpses, Whole-Bible Connections, and Theological Soundings?

What have these books brought home to you that leads you to praise God, turn away from sin, and trust more firmly in his promises?

As You Finish Studying Jonah, Micah, and Nahum . . .

We rejoice with you as you finish studying the books of Jonah, Micah, and Nahum! May this study become part of your Christian walk of faith, day by day and week by week throughout all your life. Now we would greatly encourage you to study the Word of God in an ongoing way. To help you as you continue your study of the Bible, we would encourage you to consider other books in the *Knowing the Bible* series, and to visit www.knowingthebibleseries.org.

Lastly, take a moment to look back through this study. Review the notes that you have written, and the things that you have highlighted or underlined. Reflect again on the key themes that the Lord has been teaching you about himself and about his Word. May these things become a treasure for you throughout your life—this we pray in the name of the Father, and the Son, and the Holy Spirit. Amen.